Fairy Art

This edition published by Barnes & Noble Publishing Inc.,
by arrangement with The Foundry Creative Media Company Ltd.

Publisher and Creative Director: Nick Wells
Project Editor: Sara Robson
Designer: Lucy Robins

Thanks to: Sarah Goulding, Chris Herbert, Melinda Révész, Claire Walker and Polly Willis

2006 Barnes & Noble Publishing

ISBN 13: 978 0 7607 8189 0
ISBN 10: 0 7607 8189 3

Printed and bound in China

1 3 5 7 9 10 8 6 4 2

Fairy Art

ARTISTS & INSPIRATIONS

Iain Zaczek

BARNES & NOBLE
NEW YORK

Contents

Introduction

Throughout the nineteenth century, academic painting, with its Classical emphasis, was the art of the establishment. Increasingly, though, its position was challenged by newer and more adventurous movements. The most influential of these was Romanticism. The Romantics rebelled against reason and order, the values that had defined the Enlightenment. In their place, they extolled the virtues of emotion and individualism. They still looked to the past, but they preferred the evocative tales of Arthurian legend and medieval romance to the myths of the Classical world. In addition, they developed a taste for subjects that were wild, exotic or mysterious. The genre of fairy painting fell into this category.

In Britain, the Romantic era gave rise to a revival of interest in some of the neglected areas of the nation's cultural heritage, amongst them the druids, the Celts and the fairies. The latter had attracted the interest of a number of writers, but had made no appreciable impact on the visual arts. This changed quite suddenly, due to the enterprising spirit of John Boydell. During the eighteenth century, a number of artists, led by William Hogarth, had bemoaned the lack of a

national school of painting. In particular, they resented the way that the most lucrative commissions were automatically granted to foreigners. Boydell decided to address this situation. He was rich, having made a fortune through his printselling business, and also had political clout (he became Lord Mayor of London in 1790). Using these dual assets, he commissioned the major artists of the day to produce paintings of Shakespeare's plays, displaying the results in a purpose-built gallery. Among the artists who contributed to this series were Henry Fuseli (see page 110) and Sir Joshua Reynolds, who produced fairy subjects drawn from *A Midsummer Night's Dream*.

Fuseli was fascinated by folklore and the occult and, in his paintings, he explored the darker side of the fairy tradition. His interests were shared, to a greater or lesser degree by William Blake, Joseph Paton and David Scott. Similarly, the mental instability of Richard Dadd and Charles Doyle enabled them to bring fresh insights into a subject that was, after all, governed by fantasy and the irrational.

Despite all this, it was the theatrical associations of the subject that actually led to the biggest upsurge in fairy art. The spectacular effects in William Macready's staging of *The Tempest* (1838) and Lucia Vestris's version of *A Midsummer Night's Dream* (1840), coupled with the rise of fairy subjects in the ballet, left their mark on a generation of fairy painters. Daniel Maclise, Robert Huskisson, and prior to

his illness, Richard Dadd, all produced paintings that resembled miniature stage sets. In particular, they reflected the latest advances in stage lighting. Gas-lighting was introduced in 1817, swiftly superseding the use of candles in most London theatres. Limelight was also developed at this time. Its brilliant flare could create a realistic impression of moonlight and, when used as a spotlight, it could bathe the principal characters in a radiant glow.

In John Fitzgerald, the fairy genre found its greatest innovator. His paintings owe little to literature, the theatre, or even folklore. Instead, he took the bold step of entering the tiny creatures' world and portraying them just as other fairies might see them. More than any artist since Fuseli, he created his own fantasy world. His fairies are an alien species; sometimes sentimental, though they can also be cruel. Some of them look sweet, while others resemble insect-like demons. Fitzgerald stopped painting fairy scenes after the 1860s, perhaps because the market for this type of picture had dried up. From this time on, certainly, fairy subjects were increasingly confined to book illustrations. Richard Doyle's humorous illustrations started the trend, but it was the extravagant productions of Arthur Rackham and Edmund Dulac that brought it to a splendid climax. As *The Times'* critic said of Rackham's *Peter Pan*: "the appeal again seems to be addressed to the drawing room, rather than the nursery... It will remain, we may be sure, 'downstairs', where, in fact, illustrations and text will both be best appreciated".

Even when the taste for fairy pictures declined, the tiny creatures remained obstinately in the public eye. In *Iolanthe* (1882), Gilbert and Sullivan used the framework of a fairy opera to poke fun at the House of Lords, as well as Queen Victoria's friendship with John Brown. *Peter Pan* (1904) proved a huge success on the London stage, while the controversy over the Cottingley fairies rumbled on for years. In 1917, two young girls claimed to have seen fairies near their Yorkshire home, producing photographs as evidence. Experts of every kind descended on Cottingley and the girls' claims were supported by no less a figure than Arthur Conan Doyle in *The Coming of the Fairies* (1922). The photos were eventually confirmed as fakes in the 1980s.

Like Tinker Bell herself, the fairy phenomenon has never quite disappeared. There are proprietary brands of soap and washing-up liquid named after a fairy – a reminder that good fairies liked to lend a hand with the housework. Similarly, the Brownies (the junior branch of the Girl Guides) share their name with a helpful, Scottish fairy. More recently, the Dark Lords of Sith in the *Star Wars* films were inspired by a Celtic fairy (a *sith*). Fairies continue to fascinate people of all ages, and this book looks at some of the reasons for their enduring appeal.

Masters of Fairy Art

The vogue for fairy painting grew out of the Romantic movement. This complex phenomenon encouraged artists to explore many different areas, including the cult of the individual, the spirit of rebellion, and a new, emotional response to nature. It also focused attention on the irrational. In examining this subject, painters were reacting against Classical art – the art that still prevailed in the academies – which placed a high value on reason and a sense of order.

The irrational encompassed many themes, ranging from the supernatural and the occult to madness itself. The choice of theme varied from country to country. In Spain, for example, Romantic artists such as Francisco Goya (1746–1828) painted scenes of witchcraft, while pictures of fairies were virtually unknown. Why did fairy painting become so popular in Britain and not elsewhere? The answer is Shakespeare. In the late eighteenth century, when the authorities were trying to promote a national school of British art, the depiction of Shakespearean subjects was actively encouraged. They enjoyed the same prestige as historical, mythological or Biblical themes, and were certainly preferred to other theatrical work, which was generally considered a minor, specialist field.

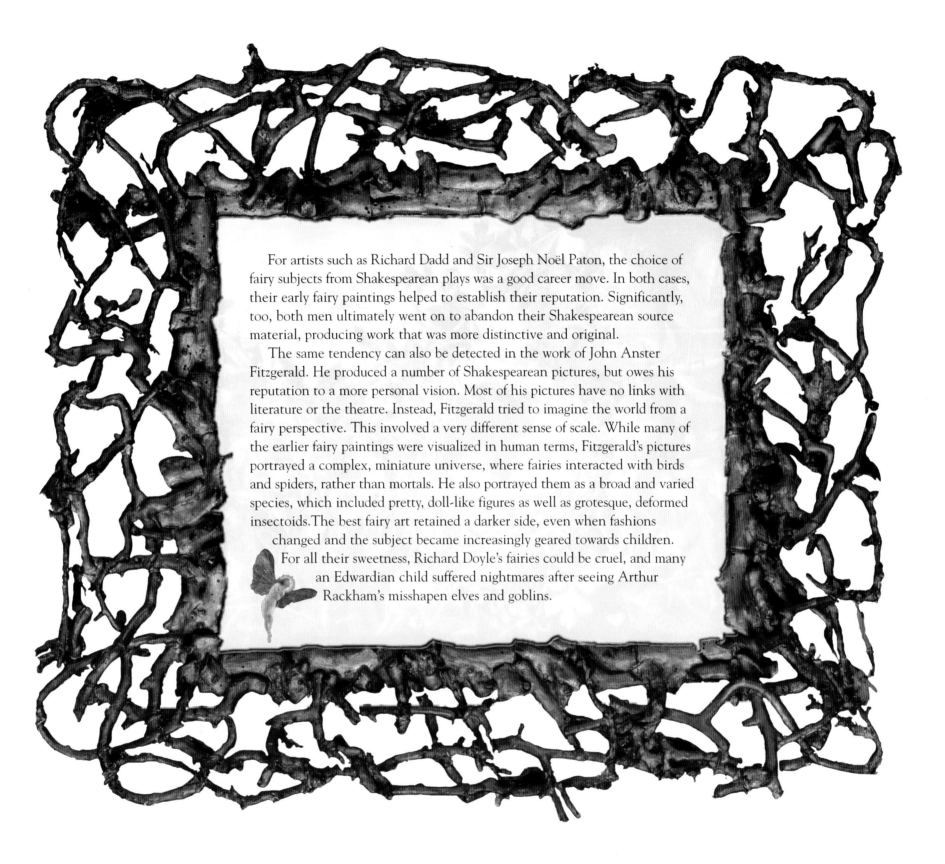

For artists such as Richard Dadd and Sir Joseph Noël Paton, the choice of fairy subjects from Shakespearean plays was a good career move. In both cases, their early fairy paintings helped to establish their reputation. Significantly, too, both men ultimately went on to abandon their Shakespearean source material, producing work that was more distinctive and original.

The same tendency can also be detected in the work of John Anster Fitzgerald. He produced a number of Shakespearean pictures, but owes his reputation to a more personal vision. Most of his pictures have no links with literature or the theatre. Instead, Fitzgerald tried to imagine the world from a fairy perspective. This involved a very different sense of scale. While many of the earlier fairy paintings were visualized in human terms, Fitzgerald's pictures portrayed a complex, miniature universe, where fairies interacted with birds and spiders, rather than mortals. He also portrayed them as a broad and varied species, which included pretty, doll-like figures as well as grotesque, deformed insectoids. The best fairy art retained a darker side, even when fashions changed and the subject became increasingly geared towards children.

For all their sweetness, Richard Doyle's fairies could be cruel, and many an Edwardian child suffered nightmares after seeing Arthur Rackham's misshapen elves and goblins.

Richard Dadd

BORN 1817 Kent, England

DIED 1886

Dadd is the best known, as well the most tragic of all the fairy painters. Born in Chatham in Kent, the son of a chemist, he trained at the Royal Academy Schools. After leaving, he joined an ambitious group of painters, known as the Clique, and enjoyed some success with his early fairy paintings, which owed much to the influence of Daniel Maclise (1806–70). Then, in 1842, he joined a fateful expedition to the Middle East. Almost immediately, his health deteriorated and he started having delusions. Things stabilized briefly upon his return but, after his picture of St George was rejected in the Palace of Westminster Competition, because the dragon's tail was too long, his condition worsened rapidly. In August 1843, he murdered his father in Cobham Park, believing that he was fulfilling a mission from the Egyptian god, Osiris.

Dadd spent the remainder of his life in mental institutions, first at Bedlam and later at Broadmoor. He was encouraged to paint, however, and in the following years produced a wide variety of work, including seascapes, historical subjects and scenes remembered from his Middle Eastern trip. His true legacy, though, came from his extraordinary fairy paintings, which displayed an intense, visionary quality that was entirely absent from his earlier work.

PUCK (DETAIL), 1841 (RIGHT)

Dadd began painting fairy pictures in the early 1840s, shortly after completing his studies at the Royal Academy. *Puck* was exhibited at the Society of British Artists in 1841, receiving considerable acclaim. In particular there was praise for the clever lighting, with the Moon behind the central figure throwing a spotlight on the action and creating a charming, dreamlike atmosphere. Together with the success of *Titania Sleeping* (see page 17) in the same year, it helped to establish Dadd as a rising star in this field. In some ways the two paintings can be seen as companion pieces, even though Puck does not illustrate a precise moment in Shakespeare's play.

Some writers equated Puck with the devil, but for Shakespeare he was 'a merry wanderer of the night', a mischievous hobgoblin who loved to lead innocent wayfarers astray. This sense of mischief is barely apparent in Dadd's painting, where the character is portrayed as an infant boy. His probable source of inspiration was Sir Joshua Reynold's (1723–92) version of the subject, which was commissioned in 1789 by Alderman Boydell, the founder of the Shakespeare Gallery. He had used as his model a small child, who turned up at the door of his studio in Leicester Fields.

Titania Sleeping, c.1841

This is one of Dadd's best-loved Shakespearean paintings, illustrating an episode from Act II, Scene II of *A Midsummer Night's Dream*. It was exhibited at the Royal Academy in 1841. The catalogue entry included the relevant quotation from the play:

> *There sleeps Titania sometime of the night*
> *Lull'd in these flowers with dances and delight.*

Behind the fairy queen the ominous figure of Oberon lurks in the shadows, waiting to cast his enchantment over her by squeezing juice from a magic flower into her eyes.

Dadd borrowed the compositional device of the fairy circle from *The Choice of Hercules* (c. 1830) by Maclise. Other elements have been linked with older sources, in particular the kneeling fairy who is said to stem from Giorgione's (c. 1477–1510) *Adoration of the Shepherds* (c. 1504). In more general terms Titania's pose resembles the popular theme of a reclining Venus, while the central group appears to be based on a Nativity group. The most unusual feature is the eerie line of dancers, who skip off downhill, disappearing into the void. *Titania Sleeping* was well received by the critics and proved highly influential on other fairy painters, such as Huskisson and Fitzgerald. This influence is all the more significant given that so much of his later work was never seen by his contemporaries.

The Attack of the Spider

Spiders were traditionally regarded as a natural enemy of most fairies. This is confirmed in the incantation that Titania's followers performed in *A Midsummer Night's Dream*:

Weaving spiders, come not here;
Hence, you long-legged spinners, hence!

Equally it is clear that the fairies found some gruesome uses for the creatures' body-parts. In his *Nimphidia*, Michael Drayton (1563–1631) described the construction of a fairy palace thus:

'The walls of spiders' legs are made,
Well mortized and finely layd.

The reason for this hostility is that in Tudor times it was erroneously believed that spiders were poisonous. The fairies in *A Midsummer Night's Dream* rarely seemed capable of anything more than mischief, but some of their kind were far more dangerous. One of their activities has left its mark on the English language. The seizure known as a stroke was originally called a 'fairy-stroke', or 'elf-stroke', because it was thought to be caused by magical arrows fashioned by elves, which pierced the skin but left no mark. Various other disabilities were also ascribed to this, ranging from lameness to wasting diseases. Similarly, ailments such as rheumatism were deemed to have been the result of fairy blows.

The Haunt of the Fairies (detail), *c.* 1841

Dadd painted two versions of this subject. The second picture, *Evening*, was roughly half the size of this one, but otherwise virtually identical. They are the least complicated of all Dadd's fairy paintings. As the sun begins to set a female fairy gathers flowers, which she weaves into a garland for her hair.

In the early 1840s Dadd produced a series of exquisitely painted, if fairly conventional, fairy pictures that established him as a leading figure in the field. His promising career was dramatically cut short, however, by the onset of mental illness. In 1842 Dadd embarked on a painting tour of the Middle East. There he worked in a frenzy, reducing himself to a state of nervous exhaustion. On his return he began suffering from delusions, believing that he was a servant of the god Osiris, charged with the task of exterminating demons. On 28 August 1843 he killed his father and fled to France. There he was arrested after trying to stab a second man and was sent back to England. Dadd spent the remainder of his life in mental institutions. He was allowed to continue painting, however, producing his greatest masterpieces during his confinement (see page 22).

Come unto these yellow sands, 1842

This is probably the finest of Dadd's early fairy pictures. It also has considerable poignancy, given that it was the last picture the artist completed before embarking on the fatal journey during which he lost his sanity.

The subject is taken from Act II of *The Tempest*. Ariel is wearing the sea-nymph costume, which renders him invisible to all but Prospero. In this guise he plays and sings the following tune:

> Come unto these yellow sands,
> And then take hands;
> Curtsied when you have, and kissed
> The wild waves whist…

Ariel's sprites dance obediently and as they do so, the storm begins to abate. Ferdinand hears their music, but sees nothing.

Dadd exhibited the picture at the Royal Academy and the Liverpool Academy, where it was shown under a different title (*Fairies holding their Revels on the Sea Shore at Night*). The critical response was highly favourable. The reviewer from the Art Union remarked that "it approaches more nearly to the essence of the poet than any other illustrations we have seen." The eerie lighting successfully conveys the stormy atmosphere, while the composition has a distinctly theatrical flavour. The sprites dance on their toes, resembling the ballet dancers in Marie Taglioni's London productions.

❧ A Fairy Verse
Full fathom five thy father lies,
Of his bones are coral made;
Those are pearls that were his eyes,
Nothing of him that doth fade,
But doth suffer a sea-change
Into something rich and strange.
William Shakespeare, *The Tempest*

The Fairy Feller's Master-Stroke, 1855–64

By common assent, this is the most complex and original of all fairy paintings. The spectator peers through a web of grasses, to witness the secret activities of a distinguished group of fairy folk. In the centre a fairy woodsman (the 'feller') raises his axe, to see whether he can split a hazelnut with one blow (a 'master-stroke'). He waits for the word from the white-bearded magician, who is running the show ("Except I tell you when, strike if you dare"). The other spectators include Oberon and Titania (above the magician), Queen Mab in her coach (on the brim of his hat), and figures from a nursery rhyme: soldier, sailor, tinker, tailor, ploughboy, apothecary, thief.

Dadd invented the subject himself, explaining the characters in a lengthy poem. He did not attempt to compose the scene, but "gazed at the canvas and thought of nothing, until pure fancy began to give form to the cloudy paint". There is no horizon, no logical sense of space and the fairies are painted in many different shapes and sizes. As a result, the picture seems airless and disorientating. The painting was not exhibited publicly until the 1930s. It was owned for a time by the poet Siegfried Sassoon (1886–1967), who donated it to the Tate Gallery in memory of three of Dadd's great-nephews, who had served with him in the trenches.

Sir Joseph Noël Paton

Born 1821 Dunfermline, Scotland

Died 1901

Paton was born in the Scottish town of Dunfermline, the son of a damask designer. He considered a career in the textile industry, working briefly in the Paisley mills, but decided to become a painter instead. He studied at the Royal Academy Schools in London, where he became close friends with John Millais (1829–96), one of the founding members of the Pre-Raphaelite Brotherhood. Paton might easily have joined this group, as he shared their taste for romantic subjects, executed in a rigorously detailed manner, but he preferred to return to Scotland, where he rapidly established himself as a fine painter of historical and mythological subjects.

Paton won great acclaim for his fairy paintings from *A Midsummer Night's Dream*, and *The Reconciliation of Oberon and Titania* received a major award in the Westminster Hall Competitions. His reputation was secured by 1850, when he was elected as a member of the Royal Scottish Academy, and Queen Victoria became a firm admirer of his work. She appointed him Her Majesty's Limner for Scotland in 1864 and knighted him three years later. Paton's last great fairy painting was *The Fairy Rade* in 1867. After this, he devoted himself increasingly to solemn religious works, which were sent on touring exhibitions, accompanied by a lecturer.

The Reconciliation of Oberon and Titania, 1847

This *tour de force* was Paton's first major fairy painting. It illustrates a scene from Act IV of *A Midsummer Night's Dream*. Oberon has reversed the effect of the magic flower, ending his wife's infatuation with Bottom. Meanwhile Puck, the grinning youth with large ears pictured to the left of the tree, has just removed his ass's head. Oberon also places a charm on the sleeping Athenians, so that they are not awoken by the fairies' celebrations. These revelries are very varied, but will shortly come to an end. To the left, dawn is breaking and the fairies must depart.

Paton's picture is remarkable for the sheer wealth of detail. He also made a significant innovation by adding a statue of Pan in the background. Pan was not only the Greek god of woods and fields, but also a personification of lust. This explains the many amorous figures in the scene, while also suggesting that Paton may have drawn some inspiration from earlier depictions of bacchanals. These wild scenes of celebration had been a favourite theme for artists such as Nicolas Poussin (1594–1665) and Titian (*c.* 1485–1576).

The Quarrel of Oberon and Titania (detail), 1849

This depicts the first encounter between Titania and Oberon in *A Midsummer Night's Dream*. He chides her for failing in her wifely duties by keeping the Indian boy from him. Titania accuses Oberon of stealing away from fairyland to play on his pipes and seduce young women, a detail that may have inspired Paton to include the statue of Pan on the right.

Paton had produced a smaller version of this scene in 1846, but this is his definitive treatment of the subject. It forms an obvious companion piece to *The Reconciliation of Oberon and Titania*. These two pictures did much to secure Paton's reputation. *The Reconciliation* won a £300 prize in the Westminster Hall Competition, while *The Quarrel* was received with great acclaim when it was exhibited at the Royal Scottish Academy in 1850. Critics were especially impressed by the amount of detail that he had managed to cram into the scene. Lewis Carroll (1832–98) reported excitedly that he counted 165 fairies when he saw the picture in 1857. Paton himself has often been described as the Scottish Pre-Raphaelite. He became a friend of John Millais (1829–96) when they trained together at the Royal Academy and, if he had not returned to Scotland in 1844, Paton would almost certainly have become a member of the Brotherhood.

Titania and the Indian Boy (detail)

In *A Midsummer Night's Dream*, a young Indian prince who has been kidnapped by the fairies is the cause of a bitter dispute between Titania and Oberon. The latter wishes to have the child as his page, but Titania refuses to part with him out of a sense of friendship. The boy's mother had been a worshipper of her cult before dying in childbirth, and she is determined to bring him up in her bower. Paton's picture illustrates this point, using a passage near the start of Act II where:

> *she perforce withholds the loved boy,*
> *Crowns him with flowers, and makes him all her joy.*

Shakespeare probably got the idea of using an Indian boy from *Huon of Bordeaux*, his source for the character of Oberon. In the book, Huon crosses paths with the fairies while he is travelling east, on his way to meet up with the fairest maid in all of India. The precise location, however, was immaterial. The main idea was to underline the supernatural powers of the fairies by showing that they could fly to the other side of the globe with ease.

✸ A Fairy Rhyme
I do wander every where,
Swifter than the moon's sphere;
And I serve the Fairy Queen,
To dew her orbs upon the green.

William Shakespeare,
A Midsummer Night's Dream

Puck and Fairies, from A Midsummer Night's Dream, c. 1850

The character of Puck was not invented by Shakespeare, but he certainly modified it a great deal. Strictly speaking he should be described as a puck, since the word actually refers to his nature. A puck was not a fairy, but a type of hobgoblin. As such, there are links with the Irish *pooka*, the Cornish *bucca* and the Welsh *pwca*. Reports of their behaviour were very varied, but in general they were mischievous rather than malicious and on some occasions they could be willing helpers. Shakespeare's puck is identified in the text as Robin Goodfellow. The surname was a deliberate piece of flattery, designed to keep in the creature's good books. In the same way, country folk often used to leave out a bowl of milk for them to curry their favour.

In Victorian art, Puck was often shown sitting on a mushroom or toadstool. This betrayed the influence of the stage, for the character often made his first appearance in this guise. This is clearly evident in Dadd's version of the subject (see page 15). Here, a fairy mimics the usual pose while his companions serenade him and Puck looks on with apparent amusement.

Oberon and the Mermaid

This scene depicts an episode from Act II of *A Midsummer Night's Dream*. Oberon is recalling an occasion, when he was sitting on a rocky promontory, watching a mermaid ride on a dolphin's back and listening to her sweet, unearthly song. During this interlude, he noticed one of Cupid's darts fall to earth and strike a flower, impregnating it with its magical qualities. Oberon decides to use the juice from this plant to make Titania fall in love with Bottom, just as if she had been pierced by Cupid's arrow.

The picture is not strictly accurate, since Puck was not present at this scene. He is relevant, however, as Oberon sends him to fetch the plant, which is shown here, next to the fairy king's leg. The same subject had previously been painted by another Scottish artist, David Scott (see page 113), though it is not clear if Paton had seen this. The principal difference between the two canvases is that Scott's version takes place at sunset, while Paton's picture is set against a moonlit panorama.

29

The Fairy Queen (detail)

This is an oil sketch for a more detailed painting of *The Fairy Queen*, which Paton completed in the 1850s or early 1860s. In the other work, it becomes clear that the figure in the background is an allegory of Night. This takes the form of a nude woman with large, black wings, who draws a veil of darkness around the reclining queen. She also scatters poppies, representing sleep. The subject is Titania from *A Midsummer Night's Dream*, shown in an episode from Act II. Once she is asleep, Oberon will anoint her eyes with magic juice. The lyre in the foreground emphasizes the Classical setting of the play, near ancient Athens.

The depiction of Titania is reminiscent of the versions by painters such as Huskisson and Simmons (see pages 114 and 123). However, it is also closely related to one of Paton's major projects of the period: *The Pursuit of Pleasure: A Vision of Human Life* (1855). In this picture Pleasure, the daughter of Cupid and Psyche, is represented by a fairy-like nude with butterfly wings.

☙ A Fairy Song

On the ground
Sleep sound:
I'll apply
To your eye,
Gentle lover, remedy.

William Shakespeare,
A Midsummer Night's Dream

The Fairy Rade: Carrying off a Changeling, Midsummer Eve (detail), 1867

This is the greatest of Paton's three major fairy paintings. The first two – *The Quarrel of Oberon and Titania* (see page 26) and *The Reconciliation of Oberon and Titania* (see page 25) – had both been based on Shakespearean themes, but this one is strikingly original. The chief sources of inspiration came from the medieval romances of Sir Walter Scott (1771–1832) and from Scottish folklore.

The title of the painting is a pun. The fairies have stolen a child, who sits on the lap of the lady on the left. At the same time, this is also a fine example of a fairy rade. This was a solemn procession, during which the fairies paraded in all their finery. Accounts of these rades were commonplace in ballads, such as *Tamlin* and *Allison Gross*. Some folk claimed to have witnessed one of these events, drawn by the eerie sounds of jingling bridles, clattering hooves and low chanting, though it was highly dangerous for mortals to spy on a rade. Paton's picture was also influenced by the revival of interest in Celtic lore, and in particular by the myths attached to prehistoric monuments and the Druids' activities at Midsummer.

A Midsummer Night's Dream, 1884

Paton's picture depicts a key episode from Act II of *A Midsummer Night's Dream*. Puck has returned from his search and hands the magic flower to Oberon. He will anoint Titania's eyes with its juice, and when she awakes she will fall in love with the first creature she sees. Although this is far less complex than Paton's principal treatments of the theme (see pages 25 and 26), it still has some unusual features. Puck, for example, is portrayed with bat wings, rather than those of a butterfly. He also wears a curious red hat, resembling the winged cap of Mercury, the messenger of the gods.

Prominent nude figures rapidly became a staple feature of this subject. Depictions of the nude were generally on the increase in nineteenth-century British art, but they were only deemed respectable in certain contexts. Links with nudes from Classical or Renaissance art were particularly desirable. These associations were not restricted to the subject matter, but also included the pose. Many artists chose to show Titania sleeping, for example, because this offered them an opportunity to echo the pose of a reclining Venus. This was one of the favourite themes of the Venetian artist Titian (*c.* 1485–1576), whose reputation soared in Britain after his *Diana and Actaeon* and *Diana and Callisto* were exhibited publicly at the start of the nineteenth century.

Fairies on a Shell

At the height of the fairy craze, many artists chose to portray a pair of fairy lovers floating downstream on a tiny vessel and it became one of the clichés of the genre. In most cases the couple were depicted on a leaf or an acorn cup. This had the dual advantage of emphasizing their diminutive stature and their rural habitat. In opting for a shell instead, Paton was betraying his Classical training. There was far less chance of coming across a scallop shell in a woodland glade, but it did underline the link with romance, as it was a traditional attribute of Venus. The goddess of love was wafted ashore on a giant shell after her birth at sea, and she was often portrayed riding in a shell-like carriage.

As a fairy artist, Paton also had the distinction of producing the illustrations for the first edition of Charles Kingsley's (1819–75) *The Water Babies* (1863). These included a striking depiction of Mrs Doasyouwouldbedoneby on the frontispiece.

John Anster Fitzgerald

Born 1832 London, England

Died 1906

itzgerald came from an unconventional background. His grandfather was an Irish adventurer, who commanded a regiment in the Dutch army, while his father was an actor and poet. His own lifestyle was scarcely less colourful. He was a habitué of the Savage Club and the London Sketch Club, where be became feted for his impersonations of famous actors, delivered in a cod Irish accent.

Fitzgerald was a versatile artist. His main income seems to have come from painting portraits, although he also produced drawings for the *Illustrated London News*. Between 1845 and 1902, he exhibited regularly at the Royal Academy, which eventually granted him a pension. It was his fairy paintings, however, that secured his reputation. Friends and critics alike described him as 'Fairy Fitzgerald', while a colleague quipped that his entire life was "one long Midsummer Night's Dream". His chief innovation was to reduce the literary and theatrical emphasis of the subject, creating instead his own, unique vision of fairyland.

The Painter's Dream, 1857

This compelling work dates from the late 1850s, when Fitzgerald produced a series of paintings on the subject of sleep and dreams. Here the artist has fallen asleep in his chair. In his dream he sees himself painting a beautiful fairy. This same portrait is shown on the right, covered by a drape, where a mischievous spirit attempts to make his own amendments to it. There are suggestions that the sleep may be drug-induced. One of the creatures offers a large glass to the artist, while the female fairy sits under a purple convolvulus, which was known for its narcotic properties. The same flower was also featured prominently in *The Fairies' Banquet* (see page 39). It is unclear whether these grotesque fairies were meant to be figments of the artist's imagination, appearing to him in his dream, or whether they were meant to be genuinely threatening him in his studio. Either way the picture makes an interesting comparison with a similar painting that Charles Doyle (1832–93), produced during his confinement in the Montrose asylum. In *Self-Portrait, A Meditation* Doyle pictured depicted himself in the company of a group of equallymenacing figures. The difference was, however, that Doyle was wide awake and the demons seemed all too real.

The Stuff That Dreams Are Made Of, 1858

In the 1850s, Fitzgerald painted a series of 'dream' pictures that are his most complex and controversial works. Here, a young woman lies fast asleep on her bed. In her dream she sees herself with a young man, standing underneath a bunch of mistletoe that is dangled over them by a grinning wraith. To the right of this romantic episode the woman can be seen again, fleeing from a goblin. In a third scene, by the window, she appears to be in the grip of the creatures, although she gazes back wistfully at her former, happy state. Meanwhile, all around the girl's bed a grotesque fairy band create a fearful din. It was well known, of course, that fairies could play a magical form of music that would not disturb the sleep of any mortal.

Fitzgerald's painting is full of ambiguities. It is clear that this is no ordinary sleep. The girl is fully clothed, wearing the same exotic attire as in her dream. There are suggestions that the dream may have been induced by narcotics. In earlier versions of the picture a goblin carries a tray of foaming drinks (still barely visible on the left) and there are medicine bottles on the table. Equally it is possible that the girl is under an enchantment, administered by the creatures in her vision.

The Fairies' Banquet, 1859

Using a mushroom as a table, a colourful array of fairies sit down to eat. The glistening fruit looks tempting, but all may not be as it seems. At the top, a purple convolvulus is prominently displayed; a flower that normally signifies sleep or death. The company looks equally mixed. Some of the fairies are undeniably sweet, but others appear demonic. Although their food always looked delicious to mortals, fairies often created this impression by using 'glamour', a form of enchantment that distorted the viewer's perceptions. Underneath this magic sheen the food might be far less enticing. Robert Herrick (1591–1674), for example, wrote that they ate:

'Beards of mice, a Newt's stewed thigh
A bloated earwig, and a Flie.

When humans did try fairy food, they usually found the taste exquisite. At the same time it could be dangerous. In Christina Rossetti's (1830–94) *Goblin Market*, Laura begins to pine away after eating some of their fruit, but she is desperate to taste it again.

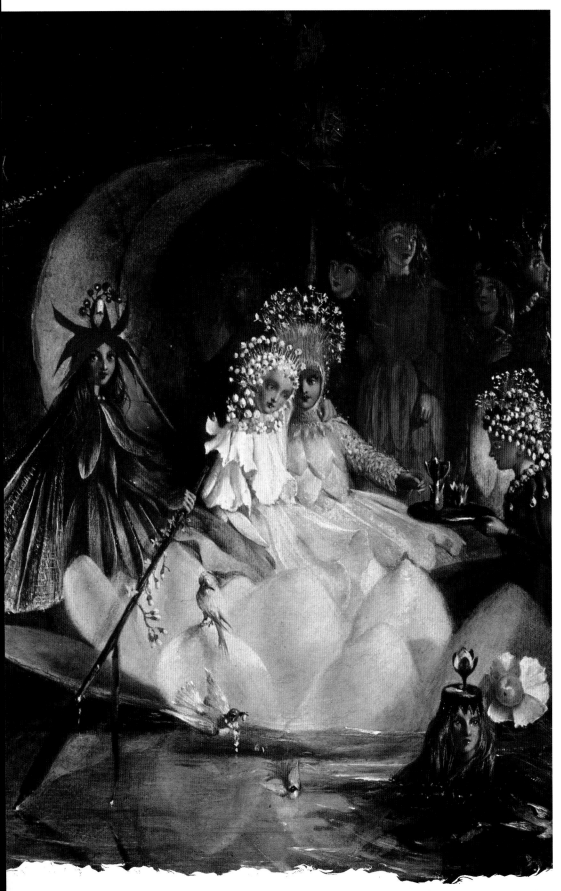

The Fairy Barque (detail), 1860

This is a variation of one of Fitzgerald's favourite themes, the fairy banquet. Here the fairy queen and her consort glide along in a giant water lily, while one of her attendants offers them sustenance. Meanwhile, the barque is gently propelled with bull-rushes by other members of her retinue.

The real star of the show is the lily itself. The flower gleams brightly and appears to be the only light source in the picture. Almost certainly this was inspired by a contemporary event, as Joseph Paxton had recently succeeded in cultivating the *Victoria Regia* (a giant water lily) in England for the first time. The feat was widely recorded in the press, and in the *Illustrated London News* there was a picture of Paxton's daughter standing on one of the huge leaves. The topicality of the subject may have persuaded Fitzgerald to exhibit the painting. Accordingly, it appeared at the British Institution in 1860, with a price tag of £35. Although the artist frequently exhibited his more conventional work, he rarely showed his fairy pictures. For this reason, no doubt, *The Fairy Barque* displays no hint of the cruelty that is often present in his paintings.

The Storm

This is an example of the one of the most popular fairy themes, where tiny creatures float downstream on a leaf or a flower. As usual, the chief attraction of the scene lies in Fitzgerald's inventive mix of creatures. His fairyland is truly a place of wonder, where pretty, doll-like humans cohabit peacefully with strange, mutated insects. More than any other fairy artist, however, Fitzgerald gives the impression that appearances may be deceptive. Here the viewer may feel empathy for the humanoids as they cling together in the aftermath of the storm, but elsewhere their behaviour is more questionable. At times they can be vicious, while their lack of emotion can make them appear sinister. It is often unclear whether the more grotesque fairies are meant to be regarded as evil or simply ugly. Fitzgerald was evidently familiar with the work of Hieronymus Bosch and Pieter Brueghel. In their work, however, the context usually offers some clues to the interpretation of the figures, but in Fitzgerald's pictures the situation is frequently more ambiguous. Even in the so-called 'dream' pictures, where the grinning spirits are usually described as tormentors, their real motives remain uncertain.

A Fairy Rhyme

A lake and a fairy boat
To sail in the moonlight clear, –
And merrily we would float
From the dragons that watch us here!

Thomas Hood,
'A Lake And A Fairy Boat'

Fairy Hordes Attacking a Bat

No artist was better at portraying the malevolent side of fairies than John Fitzgerald. Here, silhouetted against the Moon, a lone bat is ambushed by a swarm of tiny creatures wielding thorny sticks. Fitzgerald's treatment of the fairies is particularly effective. Several of the larger figures in the foreground resemble sweet-faced children, who seem too innocent to be involved in an act of such cruelty. Alongside them, however, their allies are grotesque, more like insects than humanoids.

The hostility between fairies and bats was documented by Shakespeare. In *A Midsummer Night's Dream*, Titania sent her followers off to 'war with reremice (bats) for their leathern wings/To make my small elves coats…'. This was not the only use for the creatures' hides. In his *Nimphidia* (1627), Michael Drayton (1563–1631) described a miniature palace that was made out of the body-parts of the fairies' defeated foes:

> *The Windows are the eyes of Cats,*
> *As for the Roofe, instead of Slats,*
> *Is cover'd with the skinns of Batts,*
> *With Moonshine that are guilded.*

Bats probably seemed legitimate targets, because of their associations with witchcraft and the devil.

Fairies in a Bird's Nest, *c.* 1860

Fitzgerald produced a series of paintings showing armed fairies attacking a bird. In most cases their real interest lay in capturing the nest: here, the onslaught has been successful. The bird has either fled or been killed and the victors are enjoying their spoils. Three female fairies are sleeping inside the nest, while all around them a grotesque array of creatures make sport with the bird's eggs. The presence of the sleeping figures links this painting with Fitzgerald's so-called 'dream pictures' (see pages 37 and 38). Once again, the dividing line between dream and reality is uncertain. Have the grotesque figures been dreamt up by the sleepers?

The inhabitants of Fitzgerald's fairyland come from two distinct sources. The miniature humans are not radically different from the fairies of Huskisson, Paton or Simmons. They may sometimes appear more callous, however, in their animosity towards some animals. The more outlandish creatures belong to a fantasy tradition that stretches back to the Middle Ages, when they featured in the margins of illuminated manuscripts or as gargoyles on churches. There are particularly close links with the work of Hieronymus Bosch (*c.* 1450–1516) and Pieter Bruegel (*c.* 1525-69), both of whom used the image of a deformed creature crawling inside a hollow eggshell.

Cock Robin Defending his Nest

Robins appear frequently in Fitzgerald's paintings, usually as the victims of fairy malice. Occasionally these pictures refer to the children's nursery rhyme about Cock Robin (see below), but most of the subjects came from the artist's own imagination. These showed the robin under attack, defending his nest or even as a prisoner of the fairies. The choice of bird would have seemed particularly shocking to Fitzgerald's contemporaries. The robin redbreast was very popular with the British public, often appearing on Christmas cards after these were invented in 1843. The bird was thought to be well disposed towards humans. According to an old tradition, robins would cover a corpse with moss and flowers if they found one lying in a forest. There was also a Christian connection, in that the bird is said to have gained its red markings when, during the Crucifixion, it plucked one of the barbs from the crown of thorns, spilling a drop of Christ's blood on its breast. Significantly, in Fitzgerald's picture, the fairies are attacking the robin with thorns. It was deemed unlucky to kill a robin or steal its eggs, and if a farmer did so his cows would yield blood in their milk. Otherwise the usual penalties were a broken limb or uncontrollable trembling.

Who Killed Cock Robin? (detail)

Fitzgerald was clearly fascinated by this subject, producing several different pictures on the theme. The series is unusual in a number of ways. Firstly it was rare for the artist to use material from a literary source (in this case, the title comes from a popular nursery rhyme). Admittedly he did produce a few Shakespearean pictures, but these were very much the exception to his rule. More surprising, though, is the unexpected tone of the series. Fitzgerald included robins in many of his paintings and invariably these showed the fairies acting aggressively towards the bird. Yet in the scenes that portray the death of Cock Robin, there is an unmistakeable sense of grieving. Here, for example, the two main figures on the right resemble a couple comforting each other by a graveside. This apparent inconsistency has prompted suggestions that Fitzgerald was inspired by a specific, visual source. In particular, a most convincing case has been put forward for Walter Potter's version of the theme. Potter specialized in arranging groups of stuffed animals into a tableau. His interpretation of *The Death and Burial of Cock Robin* gained widespread publicity when it was exhibited in 1861.

Ariel (detail), c. 1858–68

Fitzgerald rarely produced paintings that focused on a single figure, but he made an exception with Ariel. Shakespeare's 'airy' spirit reclines on the branch of a hawthorn tree, while exotic birds from Prospero's island flutter around him. The choice of tree was significant. According to a widely held superstition, it was unlucky to cut down hawthorns since fairies hid in them. Fitzgerald was clearly fascinated with the character as he produced another painting of Ariel, showing him trapped in the cloven pine, where he had been placed by the witch, Sycorax.

Ariel has always been a difficult character to define. Strictly speaking he is not a fairy, although his powers resemble theirs. He has been described as an elemental (it is he who conjures up the storm at the start of *The Tempest*) or a sylph (a spirit of the air). On stage he has been played by male and female actors. For Shakespearean audiences the name would also have prompted some literary associations. Uriel was the name of one of the seven principal archangels, as well as a magical spirit involved in John Dee's (1527–1608) controversial experiments. Ariel was also mentioned in the Old Testament, as a name for Jerusalem (*Isaiah XXIX*).

❧ A Fairy Verse

Weak masters though ye be – I have bedimmed
The noontide sun, called forth the mutinous winds,
And 'twixt the green sea and the azured vault
Set roaring war.
William Shakespeare, *The Tempest*

The Wounded Squirrel (detail)

Fitzgerald's fairies are often malevolent but here they demonstrate
their helpful side, tending to a sick animal. Woodland creatures were
a common feature in his pictures, but they often appeared very static,
as though they were stuffed. It is certainly possible that Fitzgerald used
stuffed animals as his models, or at least was inspired by them, as the
practice was extremely common in Victorian England. In addition,
during the 1850s and 1860s, when the artist produced most of his fairy
paintings, there was a widespread craze for an eccentric type of tableau
in which dead animals were arranged into anthropomorphic settings.

This craze was sparked off at the Great Exhibition of 1851, where
a display from Germany caught the eye. In the 'Miscellaneous
Manufactures and Small Wares' section, Hermann Ploucquet showed
A Frog Carrying an Umbrella, *The Kittens at Tea*, and *Long-tail
Teaching the Rabbits Arithmetic*. Queen Victoria described the exhibits
as "really marvellous", and within a year, some of them were featured
in a book entitled *The Comical Creatures from Wurtemberg* (1851).
Ploucquet's success seems to have inspired Walter Potter (1835–1918,
see page 45), who began exhibiting works in a similar vein.

The Wounded Fawn (detail)

Fitzgerald was a prolific painter of fairy subjects, although the quality
of his work varied considerably. When he was working in watercolour,
as here, his fairies often had a wispy, ethereal quality that emphasized
their otherworldly status. Posterity has preferred his edgier pictures
where the fairies are at war with their fellow creatures, but in Victorian
times there was a huge market for sentimental scenes such as this.

Animals often feature prominently in Fitzgerald's paintings.
This has given rise to the suggestion that he was influenced by the
contemporary taste for taxidermy. The Victorians had a morbid
fascination with the subject and examples of stuffed animals were
a common sight. They were used in scientific study, and could be found
both in museums and in the home. In this respect it may be significant
that many of Fitzgerald's pictures are an unusual shape, domed at the
top. This may reflect the influence of the bell-shaped glass cases, which
were often used for display purposes in the Victorian home. Ultimately
these derived from the Wardian case, a sealed glass case invented in
1842 by Dr Nathaniel Ward as a means of preserving delicate botanical
specimens during transportation.

Fairy Twilight

Fitzgerald ushered in a new phase in fairy painting. He removed the theatrical overtones of the subject, which had been predominant in the 1840s, opting instead to show the fairies in a rustic setting, co-existing with other woodland creatures. Often these animals appear very static, suggesting perhaps that the artist was influenced by the Victorian taste for stuffed animals. There was a particular vogue for arranging these into imaginary tableaux, but the trend also extended into other media. Some landscape photographers, for example, used stuffed animals to overcome the limitations of their equipment, which was too slow to capture animals in motion. One of the pioneers in this field was John Dillwyn Llewelyn (1810–82). His wife wrote to a friend that he was "very busy making pictures of stuffed animals and birds with an artificial landscape, in real trees, shrubs, flowers and rocks... ". Llewelyn had close links with the art world, as he was a member of the Royal Society of Arts and won a medal at the Paris Exposition Universelle of 1855, his pictures influencing a number of painters. It is quite feasible that Fitzgerald knew of his landscapes with stuffed rabbits, which were produced in the early to mid-1850s.

The Bird's Nest

The combination of birds and fairies was a perennial favourite with Fitzgerald. However, the relationship between these creatures varied considerably. Fairies were often shown attacking a bird, but here they appear friendlier. The central figure offers a bird a drink from an acorn cup, while another takes food from his mouth. In a similar scene, though, the fairies attempt to poison some birds so that they can steal their nest.

Fitzgerald's interest in birds' nests was not unusual in the mid-Victorian period. Collecting birds' eggs was a popular pastime for children and the subject was covered in illustrated books. Fitzgerald must also have been influenced by the success of William Henry Hunt (1790–1864). The latter was a still-life artist who specialized in meticulously detailed paintings of birds' nests, so much so that he gained the nickname of 'Birds' Nest Hunt'. He gave lessons to John Ruskin (1819–1900), the champion of the Pre-Raphaelites, exerting an important influence on the movement. Hunt achieved his lifelike results by using a fine brush over a ground of Chinese white, a technique that Fitzgerald also sometimes employed. The fairy painter also framed some of his pictures in a mesh of gilded twigs so that they resembled a nest. These were so fragile that few have survived, but Fairies in a Bird's Nest (see page 43) is one of these.

A Fairy Song

Oh! where do fairies hide their heads
When snow lies on the hills,
When frost has spoil'd their mossy beds,
And crystalliz'd their rills?

Thomas Haynes Bayly,
'Oh! Where Do Fairies Hide Their Heads?'

Fairies in the Snow

In many of Fitzgerald's pictures the fairies seem at war with their surroundings, doing battle with birds and insects. Occasionally, however, he painted a more optimistic scene where the attitude of the tiny creatures seemed more harmonious. This tallied with a view put forward by some writers, that the fairies belonged to a happier, bygone age, before the world became sullied by progress and materialism. No one expressed this viewpoint more forcefully than John Ruskin. In a lecture entitled 'Fairyland' he painted his own picture of this nostalgic wonderland: "There are no railroads in it, to carry the children away… no tunnel or pit mouths to swallow them up, no league-long viaducts… And more wonderful still – there are no gasworks! No waterworks, no mowing machines, no sewing machines, no telegraph poles, no vestiges, in fact, of science, civilization, economical arrangements, or commercial enterprise!".

Cat Amongst Fairies (detail), c. 1860

The treatment of fairy subjects changed dramatically in the 1860s. Earlier examples were often highly theatrical in their approach, but with the emergence of the Pre-Raphaelites, this approach began to change. When they were depicting outdoor subjects their pictures were notable for the meticulous detail of the landscape setting. This is immediately apparent in Sir John Everett Millais' (1829–96) canvas of *Ferdinand Lured by Ariel* (see page 116), where the artist spent weeks producing the background at Shotover Park, near Oxford. Despite these efforts, *Ferdinand* was ultimately judged a failure, largely because the fairy subject matter sat uneasily with the human scale of the environment. As a result, the Pre-Raphaelites rarely tackled fairy themes again. Fitzgerald solved the problem by concentrating solely on the fairy elements, but portraying them with a fine attention to detail.

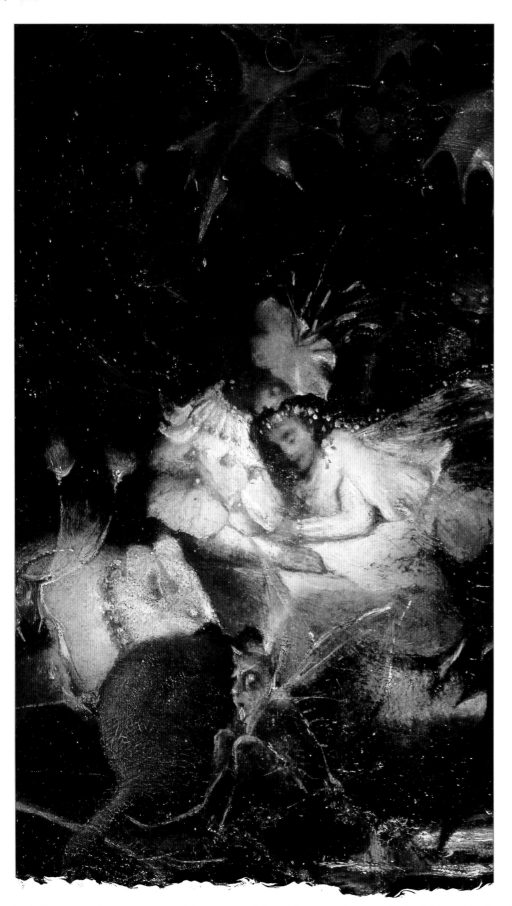

In the Fairy Bower (detail)

Unusually for Fitzgerald, this painting displays some theatrical qualities that hark back to the fairy pictures of the previous decade. A spotlight focuses on the embrace of the fairy couple, while leaving their companions in the shade. Even so, this is a comforting and harmonious scene. Although the couple are surrounded by mice and some very strange attendants, nothing threatens to disturb their sleep.

Fitzgerald's pictures were produced at a time when there was considerable concern about the future of the countryside. Political economists seemed determined to pursue the goal of progress at any cost, as the following passage illustrates: 'When we have ascertained, by means of science, the methods of Nature's operation, we shall be able to take her place to perform them for ourselves… men will master the forces of Nature; they will become themselves architects of systems, manufacturers of worlds.' Set against this remorseless desire for change and control, the certainties of the fairies existence began to seem like a fading dream.

The Enchanted Forest, c.1860

This scene is set on the margins of fairyland. The deer have come to the edge of the natural world, where they roam freely, to the start of the forest where the fairies hold sway. In making this distinction Fitzgerald was following an old tradition. By Tudor times many writers thought of woodlands as the natural habitat of fairies. In part this was due to a simple play on words. 'Wood' was a common term for 'mad'. At the same time it was widely believed that only people with heightened sensibilities, such as madmen, were capable of seeing the creatures of the spirit world. It did not take much imagination to make the connection between the two.

For the Victorians, the forest held an added significance. One of the driving forces behind the Romantic movement was a revolt against the growing mechanization of society during the Industrial Revolution. The genre of fairy painting was just one aspect of this movement. In its sphere the fairies were associated with the old, rural order that was slipping away. Their forests, wild and uncultivated, were indeed enchanted places. In contrast, other parts of the countryside were given over to railways and factories, the harbingers of the industrial age.

The Concert (detail)

In all the early reports of fairy activities, one of the most consistent elements was the emphasis on music. It played an important part both in their revels and in their solemn processions. The music itself varied considerably to suit these different occasions. Sometimes it was wild and frenetic, ideal for dancing. At other times it resembled a low chanting, echoing the fairies' ambiguous association with the spiritual world. Every commentator agreed, however, that the sound of fairy music was otherworldly and enchanting. Mortals felt drawn to it, although like the song of the sirens it was dangerous to listen to it for too long. This did not deter musicians from trying to learn its secrets. Many bagpipe and fiddle tunes are said to be based on the plaintive melodies heard by rural folk, when eavesdropping at fairy gatherings.

The vogue for fairy subjects also left its mark on contemporary music. Some pieces originated from the ballets on fairy themes, the most celebrated example being Pyotr Ilyich Tchaikovsky's (1840–93) *Dance of the Sugar-Plum Fairy* (1891–92). On a more general level, though, the trend also spawned a wide variety of other material including *The Fairy Garden* (1911) by Maurice Ravel (1875–1937) and Igor Stravinsky's (1882–1971) *The Fairy Kiss – Land of Eternal Dwelling* (1928).

The Fairy's Funeral (detail), 1864

There are many reports of fairy funerals. The most famous of these came from the poet and artist, William Blake (1757–1827). In his garden he witnessed "a procession of creatures of the size and colour of green and grey grasshoppers, bearing a body laid out on a rose-leaf, which they buried with songs, and then disappeared". Blake cited his visions as a key source for his art. He claimed to have experienced his first one at the age of eight, when he saw "a tree filled with angels" on Peckham Rye. Even so, his account of the funeral was similar to a number of others gathered by folklorists. Most of these had some features in common: the human witness was drawn to the event by the sound of a muffled bell; the body was uncovered and resembled a tiny, wax doll; and the cortège passed through a sacred place, whether a pagan site, such as a stone circle, or a churchyard. Sometimes the episode came as a warning. When the human peered closely he noticed that the corpse bore a miniature version of his own face. The notion of fairy funerals did not sit easily with another popular folk belief – namely that fairies did not actually die, but gradually dwindled away.

The Wake

This is an unusual subject for Fitzgerald, and one that reflected his Irish roots. The fairy traditions in Ireland were very different from those across the water, stretching far back in time to the island's ancient Celtic gods. The *Tuatha Dé Danaan* were said to have ruled Ireland for generations until their magical powers began to dwindle. At this point they cast a veil of invisibility over themselves and retired to the sidhe, their fairy mounds (actually prehistoric burial mounds). From there they continued to exert a telling influence over the affairs of mortals through their mystical powers. One of these spirits was the banshee (literally *bean sidhe* or 'woman of the *sidhe*'), who would utter a terrible howl to warn people of their impending doom. Sometimes when conditions were favourable, the barriers between the real and the spirit worlds fell away, enabling humans to see the fairies. The likeliest time was at *Samhain*, the festival of the dead, when the souls of the departed returned to warm themselves in the land of the living. *Samhain* was eventually adopted by Christians as All Saints' Day, and some of its traditions survived in the feast of Hallowe'en.

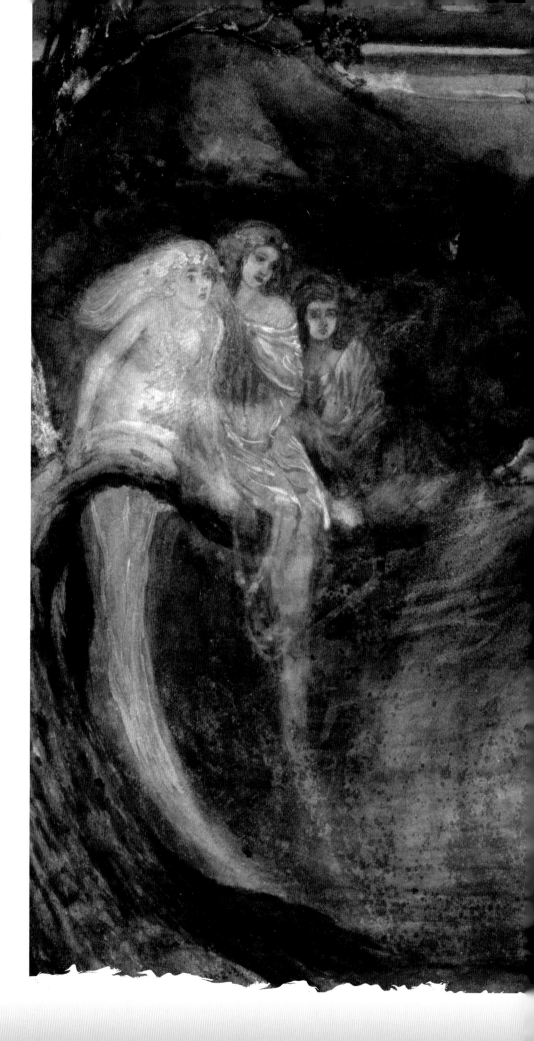

A Fairy Verse

That blessed mood,
In which the burthen of the mystery,
In which the heavy and the weary weight
Of all this unintelligible world
Is lightened –
William Wordsworth, 'Lines Written a Few Miles
Above Tintern Abbey'

John Atkinson Grimshaw

Born 1836 Leeds, England

Died 1893

rimshaw was born in Leeds and, throughout his career, the place figured prominently in his paintings. His father was employed by the Great Northern Railway and, for a time, John worked as a clerk for the same company. The decision to become an artist was a difficult one, since his parents were strict nonconformists and vigorously opposed the move. His mother even threw his painting materials onto the fire. For this reason, Grimshaw appears to have been self-taught. His earliest pictures were minutely detailed still-lifes and landscapes, painted in the style of the Pre-Raphaelites.

By the 1870s, Grimshaw had developed the distinctive nocturnal scenes that were to become his trademark. Most of these were townscapes, featuring damp, glistening roads and deserted quaysides, romantically lit by the moon and the gas street lamps. Grimshaw was fascinated by the challenge of depicting misty, atmospheric scenes with mysterious, glimmering lighting schemes and it was this, above all, which drew him to paint fairy subjects. Even though he made little attempt to exhibit his pictures, Grimshaw's work proved very popular iand was in great demand from private patrons. He was also much admired by other artists. James Whistler (1834–1903), in particular, saw affinities with his own work. "I considered myself the inventor of Nocturnes", he declared, "until I saw Grimmy's moonlit pictures."

Autumn – Dame Autumn Hath a Mournful Face (detail), 1871

During the 1870s and 1880s, Grimshaw produced a series of fairy pictures, all ostensibly drawn from literary or Classical sources. Here the title comes from an old ballad, although the artist was probably more interested in creating a wistful personification of the season itself. He saw it as a time for melancholy reflection, epitomized by such pictures as *Autumn Regrets* and *Meditation*.

Nudes are rare in Grimshaw's work, and are confined almost exclusively to his fairy pictures. Depictions of the nude could be controversial in Victorian England, but Grimshaw's paintings escaped this type of censure. This was partly due to the fairy subject matter, but also to the lyrical colouring. Problems normally only arose when a nude was painted too naturalistically, or if it was too readily identifiable with real, contemporary women. Significantly, the most famous scandal centred around John Gibson's (1790–1866) *Tinted Venus*. Gibson was the most celebrated sculptor of his day, but he aroused considerable controversy when he exhibited this polychrome statue at the International Exposition of 1862. The ancient Greeks had also coloured their sculptures, but this did not appease contemporary critics. As one pointed out, "The absence of colour in a statue is... one of the peculiarities that remove it from common Nature, that the most vulgarly constituted mind may contemplate it without its causing any feeling of a sensuous kind."

IRIS, 1876

Grimshaw painted several nearly identical versions of this picture
in the 1870s and 1880s (see pages 65 and 66). Here the subject
is Iris, the goddess of the rainbow. According to Greek mythology
she was the daughter of Pontus (the Sea) and Oceanus (the Ocean)
and was therefore closely associated with water. Her main function,
however, was as a messenger of the gods, taking orders primarily
from Hera. In fulfilling these duties she used the rainbow as a bridge
between the heavens and earth.

There is also a separate legend that links the creation of the
rainbow to an act of disobedience. At the start of one autumn, Iris
was sent down to wither the plants to mark the change of season.
As she was carrying out this task, however, she stopped to admire
a fine array of water lilies and forgot her instructions. As a
punishment for this she herself was transformed into a rainbow.
Grimshaw probably had this tale in mind when he produced his
various depictions of the goddess. The vegetation in the foreground
usually looks singed and withered (see page 65), indicating that
she had at least begun her task, while Iris herself glows mysteriously,
as if in the grip of a transformation. In addition, the entire scene
is bathed in autumnal shades of brown and gold.

> ❧ A FAIRY SONG
> Noiseless be your airy flight,
> Silent as the still moonlight.
> Silent go, and harmless come,
> Fairies of the stream:
> Ye, who love the winter gloom
> Or the gay moonbeam ...
> Gerald Griffin, 'Nocturne'

Iris, 1876

Grimshaw produced several variations of this theme. Most depict Iris, a messenger of the gods, who was turned into a rainbow after failing to wither the summer plants at the start of autumn. The painting is notable for the unusual pose of the figure as well as the eerie lighting. Iris's arms are folded across her chest and her eyes are closed as though she is asleep or dead. Prior to the nineteenth century artists had occasionally portrayed Iris in the kingdom of sleep. This occurred when Hera sent the goddess to rouse Morpheus, the god of dreams. In some variants of this picture, Grimshaw identified the figure as the spirit of the night. Here the link is that, according to Greek mythology, Sleep (Hypnos) was the son of Night (Nyx). The mysterious glow around the figure has led to suggestions that Grimshaw was influenced by the contemporary vogue for spiritualism and that the shimmering creature might actually be interpreted as a form of ectoplasm. The artist may have drawn some inspiration from this trend as the debate about spiritualism was certainly topical, but there is no evidence that he had any personal interest in the subject.

Spirit of the Night, 1879

Grimshaw painted a series of fairy pictures, all of which focus on a single, ethereal figure, hovering over an expanse of water. They fall outside the mainstream of fairy art for a number of reasons. Firstly they were created after the fashion for paintings of fairies had largely come to an end, although the tiny creatures were still popular as book illustrations. In addition his titles do not really relate to genuine fairies. Iris was a Classical deity, while Night could be interpreted as a mythological figure or an allegory. Here, though, she resembles a pantomime fairy, waving her wand. Grimshaw also painted another version of the scene, where the figure represented the goddess Artemis, gazing down at the sleeping figure of Endymion. Clearly, the subjects of these various pictures were only meant as pretexts for the depiction of an otherworldly figure, bringing a sense of magic to a nocturnal scene. Grimshaw was a genuine specialist in this field, although he usually preferred to work in a modern context, creating moonlit studies of the quayside at Scarborough or Whitby, or of the damp, leaf-strewn streets of his native Leeds.

Richard Doyle

Born 1824 London, England

Died 1883

F amed for his humorous illustrations, 'Dickie' Doyle was a popular figure in the Victorian art world. He came from a talented family. His father, John Doyle (1797–1868) enjoyed a successful career as a political caricaturist, while his brother, Charles Altamont Doyle (1832–93) was another fairy painter. Most famously of all, his nephew was Sir Arthur Conan Doyle (1859–1930), the creator of Sherlock Holmes.

Doyle's skill was evident at an early age. He was just 15 when his earliest work was published and, by the age of 18, he was already producing satirical drawings for *Punch*. He was a prolific contributor to the magazine and designed its celebrated cover, which was used from 1849 to 1956. His association with the paper ceased abruptly in 1850, however, when Doyle took exception to the anti-Catholic tone in some of *Punch's* material. After this, he devoted himself to book illustration, working for some of the leading novelists of the day – among them, Charles Dickens (1812–70) and William Makepeace Thackeray (1811–63). He is mainly remembered now, though, for his links with children's literature. As well as *In Fairyland*, he illustrated John Ruskin's fantasy, *The King of the Golden River* (1851) and an anthology of *Fairy Tales of All Nations* (1849).

The Fairy Tree, c. 1840–44

Although he is usually included in the mainstream of fairy artists, Doyle also liked to poke fun at the genre. Before all else, he was a keen observer of human foibles and a highly inventive humorist. It is no surprise therefore that this elaborate watercolour, produced at the height of the fairy craze, is actually a gentle satire on the phenomenon. In the centre, for example, the fairy king with his ridiculously long moustache is a jocular parody of noble Oberon. Elsewhere, fairies topple out of birds' nests and flower buds, while a fairy procession turns into a shambolic conga line. Most of the creatures are not really fairies, but misshapen humans. Some of the characters are comical versions of figures from everyday life: jockeys, lawyers, barbers, even a painter at his easel. Others are dressed up in costumes from pantomimes or plays. Amongst all the chaos there is a humorous performance of the balcony scene from *Romeo and Juliet*, and a grotesque version of Starveling from *A Midsummer Night's Dream*.

Baby's Dream

Sleep and dreams are common motifs in fairy paintings. There was the link with Queen Mab, the bringer of dreams (see page 111), who often put humans to sleep for sinister reasons. Ben Jonson (1572–1637), among others, noted her reputation for stealing infants:

> This is Mab, the mistris Faerie…
> This is shee, that empties cradles,
> Takes out children, puts in ladles…

Although he is probably best remembered now for his fairy pictures, Doyle was first and foremost a humorous illustrator. In his youth as well as working for several years on the satirical magazine *Punch*, designing its original cover, he also illustrated a series of books, highlighting the foibles of British society. These included *The Manners and Customs of Ye Englyshe* (1849), the *Bird's-eye View of Modern Society* (1864) and *The Foreign Tour of Messrs Brown, Jones and Robinson* (1854).

The Fairy Queen's Carriage (detail), 1870

This delightful scene comes from *In Fairyland: A Series of Pictures from the Elf World* by William Allingham (1824–89) and Andrew Lang (1844–1912), and is Doyle's most ambitious contribution to the field of fairy painting. Published in 1870, the book featured 36 coloured plates by the artist, accompanying William Allingham's verse text. Allingham probably had the harder job as, contrary to normal practice, the illustrations were completed first and he had the unenviable task of producing a series of poems that could match up to Doyle's flights of fancy.

Quite apart from the fairy elements, this picture is notable for the detailed landscape in the background. In common with many illustrators, Doyle yearned to gain acceptance in the upper echelons of the art world. Away from his work on books and magazines he tried his hand at landscape painting. Doyle based his style on that of the Idyllic school, a group of artists centred around Fred Walker (1840–75). In their paintings of rural life they abandoned the meticulous realism of Pre-Raphaelite landscapes, aiming for a more poetic effect. Doyle sent several of his landscapes to the Royal Academy, but the public and critical response to this facet of his work was disappointing.

✤ A Fairy Rhyme
I have just to shut my eyes
To go sailing through the skies –
To go sailing far away
To the pleasant Land of Play;
To the fairy land afar
Where the Little People are;
Robert Louis Stevenson, 'The Little Land'

The Triumphal March of the Elf King (detail), 1870

This is one of the most elaborate plates from *In Fairyland*, Doyle's best-known venture in this field. It depicts a fairy procession or rade (see page 80). The elf king resembles the ruler, who featured so prominently in *The Fairy Tree* (see page 69). His beard and moustache are so long that they require special attendants. Elsewhere there are instances of the spite that characterized Fitzgerald's pictures. One fairy whips a snail, while another kicks a spider and a third tugs the tail of a bird.

In Fairyland was typical of the lavish, illustrated books that were aimed at the children's market but proved equally attractive to adults. All the contributors were experienced in this field. Doyle had previously worked on James Planché's (1796–1880) *An Old Fairy Tale told Anew* (a reworking of *Sleeping Beauty*). The author, William Allingham (1824–89), was equally well known, having produced one of the most famous Victorian poems on fairies:

> Up the airy mountain
> Down the rushy glen
> We daren't go a-hunting
> For fear of little men.

Rejected!

This is another of the illustrations that Doyle produced for his most famous work, *In Fairyland*. The artist had a free hand in choosing the subjects for the pictures. The most memorable examples resembled *Punch* cartoons, in the way that they drew together several minor, comical incidents into a single scene, bustling with activity. In the remaining images, Doyle concentrated on just two or three figures. Some of these depicted fairy infants teasing a variety of insects, while others were scenes of courtship. *Rejected!* belongs to this second group. The earlier pictures showed a princely suitor, arriving at the head of a grand procession of elves, to plead his case before the princess while, in the following scene, the couple are seen flirting on a leaf.

The first edition of *In Fairyland* (1870) was accompanied by a series of verses from William Allingham. In 1884, however, the publishers decided that a prose text would be more suitable. The result was Andrew Lang's (1844–1912) *The Princess Nobody*, which concentrated on the romantic element in Doyle's illustrations. Lang had the right credentials for the job, as he also produced *The Blue Fairy Book* (1889) and *The Lilac Fairy Book* (1910).

Rehearsal in Elfland: Musical Elf Teaching the Young Birds to Sing (detail), 1870

This is another of Doyle's charming illustrations for *In Fairyland*. The fairies were known for the sweetness of their music, although more for the playing of their instruments than for their songs. There are stories about them giving some mortals the gift of music, but not birds. Instead, this is a playful reworking of the theme of the Fairy School, which was invented at the height of the fairy craze. Doyle had already parodied this in his *Fairy Tree* (see page 69), where he replaced the usual group of dainty, female pupils with a row of ungainly elves.

Doyle's picture coincided with a period of growing concern about bird welfare. By 1860 the great-crested grebe had become virtually extinct in Britain, largely because its exploitation by the fashion industry. The bird's pelt was used as a fur substitute by some couturiers, while its exotic plumage was in great demand from milliners. The Society for the Protection of Birds was founded in 1891. This received the royal seal of approval in 1899, when Queen Victoria barred certain regiments from wearing osprey plumes in their uniforms, and in 1904, when its royal charter was granted.

The Fairy Tree (detail)

In his most effective fairy pictures, Doyle managed to blend his tiny creatures into the landscape so that they seemed an integral part of the countryside. Here they congregate under the spreading roots of an old tree, watched by two young children. This was a sensible place to look, since trees were one of the principal haunts of the tiny creatures. Oaks were a particular favourite, as is confirmed in a well-known saying: 'Fairy folks are in old oaks'. In northern England they were the habitat of the sinister oak men, who preyed on unwary travellers. This gave rise to an old superstition that it was wise to ask permission before passing through an oak copse. In part these traditions probably harked back to earlier times, when the tree was regarded as sacred and was used by the Druids in their rites. Fairies were thought to be equally devoted to ash and hawthorn trees: it was deemed unlucky to cut a branch from an ash tree, and even more imprudent to burn it in the hearth. Once again this was probably a folk memory of the time when the tree was used in the fire festival of Beltane (May Day).

Dancing Fairies (detail)

Long before debates about the existence of crop circles became fashionable, country folk used to argue over fairy rings. Whenever unexplained circular markings were found in fields or meadows, superstitious locals believed that they were caused by fairies, dancing under the moonlight. More prosaically, scientists associated the circles with the roots of mushrooms and toadstools. The issue had entered the realms of folklore by the end of the Middle Ages. In *The Tempest*, Shakespeare described fairy rings as 'green sour ringlets/Whereof the ewe not bites'. This alluded to the popular belief that the presence of the fairies gave the grass a sour taste, so that sheep would not graze upon it.

As always, Doyle's principal skill lay in successfully organizing a host of tiny figures into a viable composition. This was a legacy of his days at *Punch*, when his cartoons were invariably very crowded. Unlike many other artists in this field, however, he preferred to emphasize the picturesque aspects of fairy life. Even in a nocturnal scene, there is nothing sinister or threatening about his woodland creatures.

The Fairy Dance, 1875

This type of scene became extremely popular during the heyday of fairy painting. It represents the most conventional idea of fairy revels, as they dance together happily in a circle. The fairy king surveys the entertainment from his vantage point on top of a mushroom, while his queen is resting in the foreground fanned by an attentive infant. On the right two frogs have come to join in the fun, but are soon chased away.

When fairies danced they left a pattern on the ground. In the days before crop circles became fashionable, any unexplained circular markings on the ground were often described as fairy rings. This stemmed from the tradition that fairy dances could neither be seen nor heard by humans, unless they actually stepped inside the ring. Once there, mortals were likely to be swept up in the action, dancing until they were exhausted.

Fairy Dance in a Clearing

In this spirited depiction of a fairy dance, Doyle presents the action from
the viewpoint of a secret observer, peering through the grass. The witness
has been spotted, however, for a tiny fairy in the foreground is gazing
directly at us. Secrecy was often a sensible precaution at the fairy revels,
as the dances could prove fatal for unwary mortals. While they were
cavorting with the fairies they also lost all track of time. *In Llewelyn
and Rhys*, an old Welsh folk tale on this theme, two farm labourers were
returning home when Rhys inadvertently stepped into a fairy ring, where
he promptly vanished and became caught up in their dance. Months
passed and there were whisperings that Llewelyn had murdered his
friend. Tiring of this, he returned with witnesses to the spot where Rhys
had disappeared. No one could see or hear anything until they placed
a foot inside the fairy ring, at which point they heard the sweetest music
and saw the fairies dancing. Swiftly Rhys was pulled out of the circle
and, when questioned on the matter, was adamant that he had been
dancing for only five minutes.

❧ A Fairy Song

And oft, amidst the shades of night
I court thy undulating light;
When Fairies dance around the verdant ring,
Or frisk beside the bubbling spring …

Mary Darby Robinson,
'Ode to the Moon'

A Procession of Fairies and Birds (detail), 1880

This is a fairy 'rade' or cavalcade. There were many reports of
processions such as this, particularly in Scotland and Ireland.
It is no surprise, therefore, that the most striking depiction of this
type of event came from Paton, a Scottish artist who was well
versed in local folklore. In his *Fairy Rade* (see page 32) he showed
a changeling being carried off in triumph to the fairies' home in
an ancient stone circle. Most of the sightings of fairy processions
took place on mystical dates, usually Midsummer Eve or
Hallowe'en, when fairies became visible to humans. In many of
the old folktales, the rades provided mortals with an opportunity
of rescuing loved ones who had been carried off to fairyland. In
the ballad of Tam Lin, for example, a young woman called Janet
manages to snatch back her sweetheart when a procession passes
by on Hallowe'en. The fairies do their best to prevent this by
turning Tam Lin into a snake, a bear and a red-hot iron bar, but
Janet refuses to loosen her grip and so wins the day.

The Attar Cup in Aagerup: The Moment of Departure (detail)

Doyle's painting illustrates a scene from a Danish legend, which
was published in *The Fairy Mythology* (1828) by Thomas Keightley
(1789–1872). In the story, a farmhand from the village of Aagerup
spends a night in the woods cavorting with trolls. Here, as the night
draws to a close, he mounts his horse and prepares to depart. As he
does so one of the trolls hands him a stirrup cup. The picture is
charming, although clearly Doyle had not been briefed on the nature
of trolls. Originally they were conceived as malignant giants, but
Scandinavians later saw them as mischievous dwarves. In his painting,
however, Doyle depicted them as fairies. More specifically he
portrayed them as the type of fairies that could be seen at the ballet.

In common with other art forms, ballet was affected by the craze
for fairies. *Giselle, Ondine* and *La Sylphide* all had fairy themes. Ballet,
in turn, had its own impact on the visual arts. Here, for example,
Doyle depicts the new technique of dancing on pointes. Traditionally
this innovation is ascribed to Amalia Brugnoli, but it was pioneered
in England by Marie Taglioni. She made her London debut in 1830,
appearing in Didelot's ballet *Flore et Zéphyr*.

A Fairy and a Knight (detail)

When he was working on the illustrations for *In Fairyland*, Doyle produced a range of childlike, miniature figures that, for the most part, were humorously engaged in innocent pursuits. However, the fairies who appeared in his medieval scenes were very different creatures. In physical terms, they were the same size as humans, but they often had a dark side to their nature, along with the magical powers of a sorceress. Small wonder that Doyle's knight recoils from the mysterious lady, who emerges suddenly out of a moonlit landscape.

This type of fairy was frequently known as a 'fay' or 'fée'. The term derives from the *Fatae* or Fates, the goddesses of Classical legend, who governed the individual destinies of mortals. In later romances, these were replaced by the fairy godmothers who appeared at a birth or a christening, to place either a blessing or a curse on the new arrival. In Arthurian legend, the name was almost synonymous with an enchantress. The most famous examples were Morgan Le Fay, who did her utmost to destroy the Knights of the Round Table, and Nimue, who plotted against Merlin.

A Group of Fairies Tormenting a Polar Bear

The fairies in *A Midsummer Night's Dream* were able to cross the globe at will (see page 27), so it is no surprise to find them operating in the frozen, Arctic wastes. The ferocity of polar bears was a topical subject, following Sir John Franklin's (1786–1847) disastrous expedition to find a viable sea route across northern Canada. The ships never returned and the fate of the explorers remained uncertain until a second expedition of 1858–59 discovered their skeletons. From these it was evident that the bodies had been consumed by polar bears. Sir Edwin Landseer (1802–73) produced a gruesome painting recording this event called *Man Proposes, God Disposes*, which caused a stir at the Royal Academy in 1864.

In theory fairies might attack any animal, but given that they were largely seen as a rural phenomenon most of the legends relate to farm animals. Cattle blight and swine fever were both attributed to fairies. Similarly if a cow failed to produce milk it was assumed that the fairies had stolen it. A human could also be the target of fairy malice. It was sometimes said that they mixed their cakes with human blood, while blindness was a common punishment for those who spied on fairy acts.

Arthur Rackham

Born 1867 London, England

Died 1939

Rackham was born in South London, describing himself as a "Transpontine Cockney". His talent was recognized at an early age – one schoolmaster assiduously collected the drawings he confiscated – and he trained at the Lambeth School of Art. Initially, Rackham took a job as an insurance clerk, to support himself, but he soon established himself as a full-time illustrator. At first, he worked for journalistic publications, such as the *Westminster Budget*, but swiftly made the switch to book illustration. In 1898, he was commissioned to illustrate *The Ingoldsby Legends* and, from this time onwards, his energies were mainly devoted to children's literature.

Rackham developed a unique style that blended pictorial elegance with a taste for the grotesque. He drew inspiration from Japanese prints and the linear brilliance of Aubrey Beardsley (1872–98) but, above all, from the engravings of Albrecht Dürer (1471–1528). It was the latter's influence that shone through in the illustrations for *Rip Van Winkle* (1905), the book that secured his reputation. This was followed by work on a series of children's classics, including *Peter Pan in Kensington Gardens* (1906), *Alice's Adventures in Wonderland* (1907), and *Fairy Tales of the Brothers Grimm* (1909). Rackham was well aware of the secret of his success: "I can always call up any number of... horrible beasts and hobgoblins at a moment's notice... and banish them as easily, directly after I have done with them".

American Fairies (detail), (right)

In 1905, Rackham received one of his first important commissions, when he was engaged to produce 50 colour illustrations for Washington Irving's (1783–1859) *Rip Van Winkle*. In this celebrated tale, a farmer in the Catskill Mountains falls into a deep sleep, after drinking with some ghostly companions. When he awakes, 20 years have passed and he is an old man. He then proceeds to tell a series of tall tales, drawing heavily on the rich folklore of the region. Among the supernatural beings he described were minuscule mountain men, a squaw spirit who could control clouds and stars, and of course, fairies. In this picture, Rackham portrayed the Fairies of the Catskills, 'showing that fairies are pretty much alike in America as in Europe'.

Rackham's illustrations proved a huge success. A fellow artist declared that it was "one of the most beautiful illustrated books I have ever seen... One can never in future think of *Rip* without the perfect commentary of your drawings". An exhibition of the original drawings fared equally well. This triumph launched Rackham's career, helping him to land the *Peter Pan* commission, in the following year.

✣ A Fairy Verse
O hark, O hear! How thin and clear,
And thinner, clearer, farther going!
O sweet and far from cliff and scar
The horns of Elfland faintly blowing!
Blow, let us hear the purple glens replying;
Alfred, Lord Tennyson,
'The Splender Falls'

The Guest of Honour: A Baby Attended by Sprites and Fairies, 1905

In some of his pictures, Rackham blurred the dividing line between good and bad fairies. Here a group of woodland creatures celebrate the arrival of a new baby, presumably a changeling. Some garland it with flowers, while others form a procession bringing food and drink. In certain circumstances fairies were thought to signify good luck when they visited a newborn infant.

One of Rackham's greatest assets was his ability to produce a never-ending range of fairy people. His elves and goblins, with their pointy ears and noses and their churlish expressions, managed to appear humorous, whilst also remaining grotesque enough to frighten small children. The scariest components of his pictures, however, were his trees. These often seemed to come alive, with branches like clawing arms and snarling faces appearing in the bark. In this painting, Rackham's inspiration came from the engravings of his favourite draughtsman, Dürer.

Fairies Dancing (detail)

In the Spring of 1905, following the phenomenal popularity of his *Rip Van Winkle* illustrations, Rackham was offered a lucrative commission to work on J.M. Barrie's (1860–1937) tale of *Peter Pan*. The immediate stimulus for the new publication was the success of the stage play, which had opened in London in 1904. The full title of this, the best known version of the story, is *Peter Pan, or The Boy Who Wouldn't Grow Up*. It was eventually published in book form in 1911, under the title of *Peter and Wendy*. Rackham, however, was hired to work on an earlier version of the tale. This had originally been published in 1902 as *The Little White Bird* – so-called because of the myth that newborn babies could fly like birds. This was reissued in 1906 as *Peter Pan* in *Kensington Gardens*, complete with Rackham's illustrations. It was a much simpler tale, recounting Peter's experiences in Kensington Gardens, where he lived after flying away from his home. Rackham preferred this version of the story, partly because it included far more fairies. In the stage play there was just one – Tinker Bell.

The Fairies Have Their Tiff With the Birds, 1906

Rackham made a practice of exhibiting the original drawings for his illustrations at the Leicester Galleries, timing the show to coincide with the publication of the book. Apart from the sale of the drawings themselves, these occasions also gave him the opportunity to meet new clients. In 1905, for example, the Leicester Galleries arranged a meeting with Barrie, who promptly commissioned the artist to produce the illustrations for his *Peter Pan in Kensington Gardens* (1906). This delightful scene is drawn from that series, which was published in the following year. As usual the critics were full of enthusiasm for the artist's efforts.

As one commented, "Mr Rackham seems to have dropped out of some cloud in Barrie's fairyland, sent by providence to make pictures in tune to his whimsical genius". It was unusual for Rackham to be able to talk directly to one of his authors and the two men certainly enjoyed a cordial, working relationship. Even so, Rackham was disappointed that in the final version of his tale Barrie chose to transfer so much of the action to Never-Never land. "I think Never-Never lands are poor prosy substitutes for Kaatskills (Catskills: Rackham had just been working on *Rip Van Winkle*) and Kensingtons, with their stupendous powers of imagination. What power localising a myth has." As a result, Kensington Gardens featured prominently in his illustrations.

Peter Pan is the Fairies' Orchestra, 1906

This is another of the set of illustrations that Rackham provided for
Peter Pan in Kensington Gardens. Modern readers may visualize Peter
as an older boy and, on stage, he is often performed by an adult.
In the earliest version of the story, however, he was an infant, who
flew away from home when he was just a week old. He lived in
Kensington Gardens, in the centre of London, where he befriended
the birds and the fairies. He was particularly popular with the latter,
because the music he played on his pipes was ideal for dancing.
Peter's choice of instrument is significant, hinting at the origins of
his name. Pan was a Classical god, half-goat and half-man, who lived
wild in the woodlands. He invented the reed pipes and on these, he
played haunting melodies, which charmed the nymphs of the forests
and streams. Peter's name came from Peter Llewelyn Davies, one
of the sons of a neighbouring family. Barrie befriended them and
eventually became the children's guardian, after their parents died.
The story developed from the games that the boys played in their
local park – Kensington Gardens.

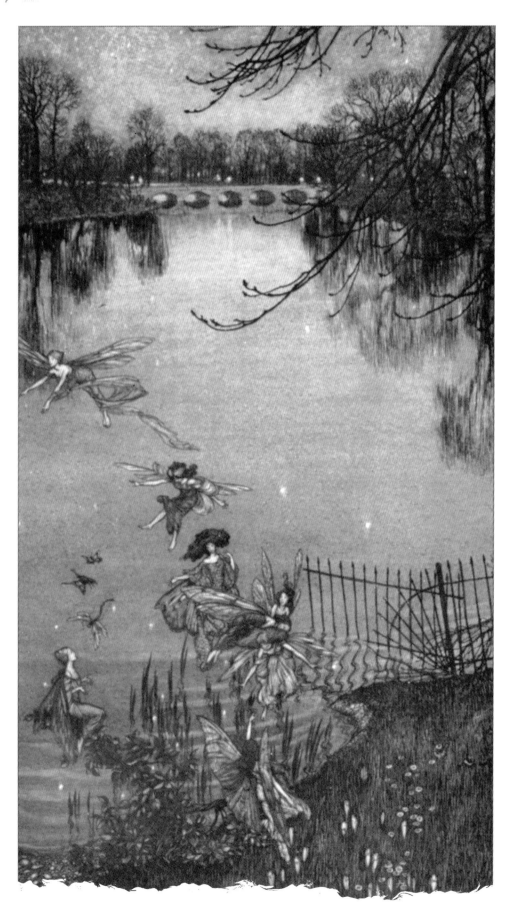

Fairies at the Serpentine

This is probably the most celebrated of Rackham's illustrations for *Peter Pan in Kensington Gardens*. It accompanies the following passage: 'The Serpentine is a lovely lake and there is a drowned forest at the bottom of it.' The beauty of the picture reinforces Rackham's belief that fantasy works best, when it is grounded in reality. The cavortings of the fairies seem all the more remarkable, because they are set against a backdrop that is instantly recognizable to most Londoners. The gaslights in the distance, which trace the course of the road across the bridge, add an extra dimension to this effect. Rackham's viewers might easily have associated these with other fairies since, in the Edwardian theatre, these minuscule creatures were often represented by tiny spotlights reflected off mirrors. The artist took great pains to ensure that the settings for his illustrations were convincing. He went on regular sketching expeditions to Kensington Gardens, often taking his young nephew with him. The lad remembered these trips with great affection, declaring that his uncle "became in my eyes a wizard who, with one touch of his magic wand, would people my imagination with elves, gnomes and leprechauns".

Fairies in their Underground Homes (detail)

This illustration, taken from *Peter Pan in Kensington Gardens*, demonstrates Rackham's abiding fascination with trees. His nephew, Walter Starkie, recalled that when he joined his uncle on painting expeditions in the gardens: "He would make me gaze fixedly at one of the majestic trees and tell me about... the little men who blew their horns in elfland. He would say that under the roots of that tree the little men had their dinner and churned the butter they extracted from the sap of the tree. He would also make me see... a little magic door below the trunk, which was the entrance to Fairyland...".

This passage highlights Rackham's extensive knowledge of fairy folklore, since there were many ancient traditions suggesting that Fairyland was located beneath the surface of the earth. In the twelfth century, for example, Ralph of Coggeshall described a magical, subterranean realm in his tale of *The Green Children*. They reached the place through a long cavern, emerging into a land where there was 'neither sun nor moon, but a perpetual dim light, like that before dawn'.

Autumn Fairies, 1906

This is another illustration taken from the 1906 edition of *Peter Pan in Kensington Gardens*. It depicts a passage where the narrator explains how fairies hide themselves from humans. One of their most effective ploys was to disguise themselves as flowers. They tailored their clothes to resemble everyday plants, altering them to suit the changing seasons. Hyacinths and crocuses were their favourite blooms, but they found the colours of tulips far too garish.

In this scene, they are mimicking the actions of autumn leaves, dancing around in the breeze. When tackling pictures of this kind, Rackham always tended to draw the background first, adding in the figures at the final stage. Although he planned out a rough idea of the composition, he never produced detailed studies, preferring to paint quickly and spontaneously. This process could be entertaining to watch. A friend remarked that he resembled a goblin "hopping about the studio with a palette on one arm, waving a paintbrush in his hand".

Fairies Weaving Curtains from Leaves

This is another picture that Rackham provided for Barrie's *Peter Pan in Kensington Gardens*. When the author wrote to the artist in 1906, congratulating him on the plaudits that his work had received, he cited it as one of his favourite illustrations, together with the *Fairies at the Serpentine* (see page 90) and *The Fairies Have Their Tiff With the Birds* (see page 88). Rackham, for his part, was also a great admirer of Barrie's writing – he named his cat 'Jimmie', in his honour. Nevertheless, he was disappointed at the way that Barrie altered the setting in his stage version of the story. Its exotic touches, with pirates, Red Indians and Never-Never land, proved hugely popular with contemporary audiences, but Rackham preferred the sense of place, which Kensington Gardens had provided. Despite this, he was able to console himself with the financial rewards of the venture. The success of *Rip Van Winkle* had enabled him to raise his prices. He charged five guineas for each illustration, but retained the original drawings. When these were exhibited, they raised a further £1850 – a staggering sum at that time.

A Fairy Rhyme
Deep in the wood's recesses cool
I see the fairy dancers glide,
In cloth of gold, in gown of green,
My lord and lady side by side.
But who has hung from leaf to leaf,
From flower to flower, a silken twine –
Dora Sigerson Shorter, 'The Watcher in the wood'

Twilight Dreams

The rampant success of *Peter Pan*, in all its forms, proved a mixed blessing for Rackham. In 1908, a new theatrical version of Barrie's story – *Peter and Wendy* – proved a hit on the London stage. Its continued popularity led to the publication of a new edition of the text in 1911, with illustrations by F.D. Bedford. This in turn prompted Rackham's publishers to recycle his old pictures from 1906 in two new formats – a reduced version of *Peter Pan in Kensington Gardens* and a *Peter Pan Portfolio*, containing enlarged reproductions of some of the original images. Rackham was horrified by both projects, largely because of the poor quality of the reproductions and because some of them had been cut down. Even so, he did consider adding some new illustrations to the original series. *Twilight Dreams* was initially designed to serve as the endpapers for the 1912 edition of *Peter Pan in Kensington Gardens*. After reflection, though, he held it back for an exhibition of his work in the following year.

Fairy Attendant, 1908

This is one of the most charming pictures from Rackham's
contribution to the 1908 edition of *A Midsummer Night's Dream*.
It shows a tiny attendant from Titania's retinue struggling to carry
a bag of berries to Bottom. Over the years, Rackham worked on four
different editions of the play (see page 102), but the 1908 version is
widely acknowledged as the finest. This may well be due to the fact
that it was produced at the happiest and most successful period in
his career. The popularity of *Rip Van Winkle* and *Peter Pan in*

Kensington Gardens had brought him international renown, while
his private life was in a blissful state. He had married Edyth Starkie
in 1903 and his daughter, Barbara, was born while he was working
on the Shakespeare illustrations. Rackham was equally content in
his studio, "a most delightful place, cool, airy and quiet", lined with
well-stocked bookcases containing "volumes of fairy lore, ancient
and modern", where he welcomed visitors at any time. The happiness
of his domestic situation was mirrored in his illustrations for the
Dream, where dainty fairies and children far outnumber his usual
array of goblins and witches.

A Fairy Stealing a Child (detail), 1908

This delightful picture is one of the memorable set of illustrations, which Rackham produced for the 1908 edition of *A Midsummer Night's Dream*. In the original story, the theft of an Indian boy provoked a quarrel between Oberon and Titania, although the abduction itself played a comparatively minor role in the action. Rackham enjoyed complete freedom when choosing which scenes to illustrate, however, and he chose to devote several pictures to the theme of stolen children.

In spite of the serious subject, there is nothing remotely menacing about any of the kidnapping pictures. Here, the abduction has been turned into an adventure, with the child taking delight in its spectacular flight over a panoramic landscape. In part, this exhilarating tone was due to the artist's personal circumstances. In 1904, the Rackhams' first child was stillborn. This tragedy clouded all the successes, which Arthur achieved over the next few years. Then in January 1908, his wife gave birth to a daughter, Barbara. Rackham was overjoyed and drew the baby constantly, including her in his work whenever possible.

Fairies on the Shore (detail)

This is another illustration that Rackham produced for the 1908 edition of *A Midsummer Night's Dream*. It shows Titania and her fairy companions lavishing attention on the Indian boy, whom she refuses to hand over to her husband. Instead, she 'crowns him with flowers, and makes him all her joy'. This theme of maternal affection held particular significance for Rackham, since his wife had just given birth to their first child (see page 97). He used the baby girl as a model in many of the illustrations in this series and even depicted her first toy – a woollen ball – hanging from the corner of the cradle in *Fairies Peep at a Baby* (see below).

Earlier fairy artists had often portrayed similar scenes, showing fairies 'entertaining' a stolen child. These pictures were rarely as innocent as they seemed. Fairy food and fairy music both had magical qualities, that could entrance mortals and hold them captive. Fitzgerald's depiction of a fairy banquet (see page 39) offers a vivid demonstration of the way that fairy food could appear both tempting and sinister. By Rackham's time, this air of menace had disappeared.

Fairies Peep at a Baby (detail), 1908

This is another of Rackham's illustrations for the 1908 edition of *A Midsummer Night's Dream*, published by William Heinemann. It relates to a line near the start of Act V ('...almost fairy time') and hints at the theme of abduction. According to popular superstition, fairies would often creep into an unguarded house at night, to steal an infant from its crib and leave a changeling in its place. They had the power to kidnap humans of any age – there are stories of adults being carried off, when they stepped unwarily into a fairy ring – but young, unchristened children were always preferred, because they lacked the benefit of spiritual protection. There were various remedies for this. The 'little pagan' would be protected if a pair of open scissors, forming the shape of a cross, was hung above the cot, or if iron horseshoes were placed at the entrances to the baby's room.

The decor of this chamber is a fine piece of invention on Rackham's part. The play was set near ancient Athens, but the artist decided to translate this to Shakespearean times, using Tudor furniture and costumes.

Arthur Rackham

The Meeting of Oberon and Titania (detail)

Rackham produced this sparkling scene for the 1908 edition of *A Midsummer Night's Dream*, although in the end it was not used in the final version of the book. It depicts precisely the same episode that Paton had depicted in 1849 (see page 26), underlining the seismic changes that had taken place in the field of fairy painting during the intervening years. With their fine clothes and their regal airs, Rackham's royal couple are the stuff of pantomimes and fairy tales, quite unlike the nude, Classical figures of Paton. More significantly his fairies are well-mannered children, content to hold lanterns and carry their masters' trains, while Paton's creatures cavort lustily in the undergrowth.

Shakespeare derived his fairies from a number of different sources. Oberon stems from *Huon of Bordeaux*, a thirteenth-century romance that was first translated into English by Lord Berners (*c.* 1469–1533). In this, Huon performs a number of seemingly impossible tasks, with the magical assistance of the fairy king. Titania, meanwhile, came from a Classical source. Ovid (43 BC–AD 17) had used the name to describe a number of female woodland spirits who were descended from the Titans, an ancient race of Greek gods. Puck, or Robin Goodfellow, was well known from English folklore, but Shakespeare may have found additional information in Reginald Scot's (*c.* 1538–99) *Discoverie of Witchcraft* (1584).

Fairy Music (detail)

This scene depicts one of the many fairy interludes, which Rackham produced for his sumptuous 1908 edition of *A Midsummer Night's Dream*. As always, when working on a project of this kind, the development of Rackham's ideas can be traced in his sketchbooks. In his 1908 book, he devoted no fewer than 84 pages to studies for the Shakespeare play. From these, it is clear that he did not attempt to provide an ordered, conventional illustration of the text. Instead, he settled on a few favourite passages, using them as a launchpad for his own ideas. He admitted to a friend that his publications were "really rather to be regarded as bound up portfolios of pictures... They are ungainly books". Rackham never discarded his old sketchbooks, but continued to use them as source material for other commissions. In this instance, he was clearly very proud of his elvish cellist, for he used him again in a different set of illustrations, produced for the 1928 edition of *A Midsummer Night's Dream*. There, he appeared in the border of *The Fairies Sing*, which accompanied the passage where Titania's fairies lull her to sleep.

A Midsummer Night's Dream, 1908

In 1936 an American publisher asked Rackham which of Shakespeare's plays he would prefer to illustrate. In response, the artist sent him a short list, emphasizing that *A Midsummer Night's Dream* would certainly be his first choice. In the event, Rackham produced illustrations for no fewer than four different editions of the work. In 1899 he provided two pictures for a version of Lamb's *Tales from Shakespeare*, and in 1908 the finest and most influential set of designs appeared in the Heinemann edition. A third collection was commissioned in 1928 by the New York Public Library, and finally in 1936 Rackham produced a new set of pictures for George Macy of the Limited Editions Club.

The sumptuous 1908 book went down extremely well with the public. Three months after publication the entire de luxe edition had sold out, along with more than half of the trade copies. The reviews were glowing. "This is the handsomest version of *A Midsummer Night's Dream* we have ever handled", wrote one critic, while another described it as "a delightful land of make-believe". As always, the only problem was that the illustrations were clustered together at certain points of the text. Rackham always chose the lines that he wanted to depict, so on this occasion he produced five images for 26 consecutive lines of text, describing the fairy interlude in Act II.

The Fairy Ring

When quizzed about the Shakespeare plays that he would most like to illustrate, Rackham placed *The Tempest* second only to *A Midsummer Night's Dream*. His opportunity came in 1926, when he was commissioned to work on a version of the text for William Heinemann. Not surprisingly, the artist chose to concentrate heavily on the fairy elements in the story. Here, he depicts a passage at the start of Act V, where Prospero summons up the elves and spirits that 'by moonshine do the green sour ringlets make' (see page 76). According to popular superstition, these 'ringlets' were caused by dancing fairies.

During this period, landscapes featured prominently in Rackham's pictures. This followed his move to the countryside, when he left London and settled in a village near Arundel. The artist confirmed in a letter that this particular scene shows the area around his new home, in the heart of the South Downs. The chalk pits at Amberley are clearly visible in the background.

A Fairy Verse

Ye elves of hills, brooks, standing lakes, and groves,
And ye that on the sands with printless foot
Do chase the ebbing Neptune, and do fly him
When he comes back; you demi-puppets that
By moonshine do the green, sour ringlets make
Whereof the ewe not bites;

William Shakespeare, *The Tempest*

Fairies Picking Apples

Rackham produced this picture for *A Dish of Apples*, an anthology of poems by Eden Phillpotts (1862–1960). He was a prolific author, who produced over 200 books, many of them about Dartmoor, where he lived in seclusion for much of his life. The illustrations were finally completed in 1921, after Phillpotts had sent a stream of importunate letters to the artist. He later apologized, after learning that both Rackham and his wife had been unwell: "I am much concerned to know that Mrs Rackam has been ill... I am venturing to send her a pound of Devonshire cream...".

For this image, Rackham recycled some elements from *Windfalls*, a watercolour dating back to 1904, although he toned down the grotesque appearance of the elves. He also took the opportunity to depict some of the trees in his new garden at Houghton. These included a large apple tree, situated next to his studio barn. It fell down shortly after work on the book was finished, when a large cow leaned against it.

The Pert Fairies and the Dapper Elves (detail)

Rackham's picture illustrates a few lines from John Milton's (1608–74) *Comus*, a masque that was first performed at Ludlow Castle in 1634. Masques were lavish spectacles in which music and dance featured prominently, but *Comus* was also a dark tale of a struggle between good and evil, featuring a moral lesson about the dangers of eating fairy food. Milton's roots were in Oxfordshire, where he steeped himself in the local fairy traditions.

Elves appear in many different guises in fairy painting. The creatures originated in Scandinavian mythology, where from an early stage a distinction was made between light elves and dark elves. The former were generally harmless, while the latter could be far more sinister. In Britain the meaning of the word was equally varied. For Shakespeare the term was virtually synonymous with diminutive fairies, but in Scotland it was usually reserved for larger ones. Their behaviour was equally varied. Some elves could be evil: kidnapping humans, stealing cattle and ruthlessly taking revenge for any perceived slights against them.

Other Artists
&
Influences

During its rise to popularity, the overriding influence on British fairy painting came from literature and, in particular, from Shakespeare. Most artists, however, were less interested in the fine detail of the text, than in the way that the plays looked, when they were performed on stage. Accordingly, the preference for lyrical, moonlit scenes reflected the latest advances in theatrical lighting. Similarly, the copious depictions of fairy dancing and fairy concerts were prompted by the fact that A *Midsummer Night's Dream* was usually performed as a musical extravaganza with balletic interludes. Indeed, the strong links between fairies and dancing were maintained throughout the century. Significantly, when J.M. Barrie was musing over the name for the fairy in *Peter Pan*, he initially thought of calling her Tippy Toe, rather than Tinker Bell.

Alongside their literary sources, artists also drew inspiration from some of the popular traditions concerning fairies. Their favourite theme, perhaps, was that of the changeling. It is easy to see how this legend evolved. If a newborn child was a disappointment in any way – if, for example, it was sickly, unsightly, or did not resemble a husband closely enough – then it was all too easy to blame it on the fairies, claiming that they had stolen the real

child and left a defective substitute behind. Many fairy superstitions were based on the same principle, of explaining away uncomfortable truths: a mysterious illness, unseasonal weather, an outbreak of cattle blight, or an untimely death.

Sometimes, literary and mythical sources were combined. Many of the fairy stories that appeared in illustrated children's books were originally folk tales. They had been passed down orally, from generation to generation, until they were finally written down. The Grimm brothers were pioneers in this field. They travelled around Germany collecting material. Some of their best stories came from an old soldier, who recited them in exchange for several pairs of trousers.

The taste for fairy lore was also stimulated by new attitudes towards nature. The Romantics looked at it with new eyes, following William Blake's famous exhortation 'To see a World in a Grain of Sand, And a Heaven in a Wild Flower'. They also viewed it nostalgically, in the wake of the Industrial Revolution, which brought workers to the towns and created immense upheavals in the countryside. Fairies, it seemed, were part of a disappearing, rural tradition, and it was important to capture this on canvas, before it vanished forever.

Literature

hakespeare's influence on fairy painting was enormous, although the material was confined almost exclusively to two plays: *A Midsummer Night's Dream* and *The Tempest*. Even here, his interest in the subject should not be exaggerated. Ariel and Caliban are not fairies, strictly speaking, while the fairies in *A Midsummer Night's Dream* were essentially a comic device, designed to facilitate the plots involving Bottom and the lovers. Shakespeare drew his information on the creatures from a wide variety of sources, but interpreted them very freely, making his fairies far more benign than their folklore counterparts.

Shakespeare was by no means the only British author to mention fairies – they feature, among others, in the work of Geoffrey Chaucer (c. 1343–1400), Edmund Spenser (1552–99) and John Milton (1608–74) – but their work was rarely illustrated by artists. It was only with the advent of children's literature in the nineteenth century that fairies made an artistic comeback. Initially, children were fed a diet of moralizing or 'improving' literature, but by the middle years of the century fantasy had become more popular. The fairy tales of Hans Christian Andersen (1805–75) and the Brothers Grimm were particular favourites, as were the whimsical works of Edward Lear (1812–88) and Lewis Carroll (1832–98).

Henry Fuseli

Born 1741 Switzerland

Died 1825

Titania and Bottom, c. 1790

In 1786 Fuseli was invited to a dinner, with a group of other artists, by John Boydell (1719–1804), the future Lord Mayor of London. There Boydell proposed the foundation of a Shakespeare Gallery, with contributions from the leading painters of the day. This picture was one of a number on Shakespearean themes that Fuseli created specifically for the project.

Titania and Bottom was inspired by the characters from *A Midsummer Night's Dream*, but does not illustrate any particular scene from it. Instead Fuseli used the subject as a launching pad for his own imagination, producing a far darker vision of fairyland than any devised by his Victorian successors. In the centre, in a pose borrowed from Leonardo's (1452–1519) *Leda*, Titania waves her wand aloft while her attendants lavish attention upon Bottom. Around them a macabre array of spirits loom out of the darkness. On the right, a woman holds a short old man on a leash, symbolizing the triumph of beauty over reason. Beside her a hooded night-hag displays a hideous changeling, which she will leave in the place of a stolen baby. On the left a group of monstrous chidren assemble, headed by a sinister little girl with butterfly wings for ears.

George Cruikshank

Born 1792 London, England

Died 1878

Queen Mab (detail)

Cruikshank's painting is a very literal depiction of the fairy, as described by Shakespeare in *Romeo and Juliet*. In the play, Mercutio refers to Queen Mab as:

> *In shape no bigger than an agate-stone*
> *On the forefinger of an alderman,*
> *Drawn with a team of little atomies*
> *Athwart men's noses as they lie asleep*

In Tudor times, Mab was known as the bringer of dreams, hence why she drives her carriage across the heads of sleeping humans. However, Mercutio dismisses her as a piece of superstitious nonsense and, significantly, she does not figure in the play. Apart from anything else, this underlines the enormous impact that Shakespeare had on fairy traditions. Prior to *A Midsummer Night's Dream*, Mab had been regarded as the Queen of the Fairies, but, with her diminutive size, she was rapidly supplanted by Titania. The name remained in popular usage: she features in the writings of Michael Drayton (1563–1631) and Ben Jonson (1572–1637), but her powers were greatly diminished. She was largely reduced to turning milk sour and leading travellers astray. Yet she probably originated as a god. Many authorities have linked Mab with Medb or Maeve, the Celtic goddess of war, who dealt death and destruction to unwary humans.

&❧ A FAIRY VERSE

Since once I sat upon a promontory,
And heard a mermaid on a dolphin's back
Uttering such dulcet and harmonious breath
That the rude sea grew civil at her song ...

William Shakespeare, *The Tempest*

David Scott

Born 1806 Edinburgh, Scotland

Died 1849

Ariel and Caliban (detail), 1837

During his brief career, David Scott produced work of startling originality. None was more remarkable than the two Shakespearean pictures, which he exhibited at the Royal Scottish Academy in 1838: *Puck Fleeing before the Dawn* and *Ariel and Caliban*. The latter depicts Prospero's two contrasting servants in *The Tempest*. Ariel is the ethereal spirit, whose nature and powers transcend the realm of earthly affairs. He hovers effortlessly in the air, and his foot brushes carelessly against Caliban's brow, emphasizing his innate superiority. Caliban, meanwhile, is ugly and earthbound. He may have greater brute strength, but he gazes up jealously at Ariel, longing to share his fairy-like state. Under his arm he carries the bundles of firewood, which Prospero has ordered him to gather, while in his hand he grips an adder, that his cruel master has sent to 'hiss me into madness'. By his knee, a squat toad underlines his lowly status, contrasting with the delicate butterfly that flutters beside Ariel.

Scott's pictures were greeted with bemusement by the critics – one even claimed that he had the "imagination of madness". Nevertheless, they were purchased by the Society for the Promotion of Fine Art, and have since been likened to the visionary creations of William Blake.

Oberon and Puck Listening to the Mermaid's Song (detail), c. 1837

Scott's picture illustrates an interlude from Act II of *A Midsummer Night's Dream*. During this interlude, Oberon notices one of Cupid's arrows going astray and striking a tiny flower, presumably the plant on the picture's left. The fairy king would use this enchanted bloom to cast a spell over his wife. The image of the mermaid may have been suggested by the legend of Arion, a bard who escaped from pirates on a dolphin's back.

David Scott was the elder brother of William Bell Scott (1811–90), also an artist. David hoped to earn a reputation as a history painter, but his ambitions were never fulfilled. Instead he is best known for the bold colouring and imaginative vision of his Shakespearean fairy pictures. In *Puck Fleeing before the Dawn* (1837) he portrayed the creature hurtling through the air like a cannonball, while his monstrous depiction of Caliban has never been bettered.

Robert Huskisson

BORN 1819 England

DIED 1861

The Midsummer Night's Fairies, 1847

Huskisson exhibited this picture with an unwieldy title, which included a misquotation from *A Midsummer Night's Dream*:

> *There sleeps Titania sometime of the night,*
> *Lull'd in these flowers with trances* [instead of 'dances'] *and delight…*

The picture was shown at the Royal Academy in 1847 where it was warmly received. One critic even remarked that the painter was "destined to play a premier role in British art". This optimism must have seemed well founded when the picture was bought by Samuel Carter Hall, a highly influential figure in the art world.

In creating this picture Huskisson was undoubtedly influenced by Dadd, who had exhibited his own version of the theme six years earlier (see page 17). As in that picture the spotlight is on Titania, who reclines in her bower in a pose borrowed from Giulio Romano's (c. 1499–1546) *Sleeping Psyche*. Behind her, the gigantic figure of Oberon lurks in the shadows, while Puck flies towards the fairy queen ready to anoint her eyes with the magic juice. The most original feature is the painted arch, which features the figures of Bottom and the Athenian lovers who lie sleeping, perhaps even dreaming the action that is taking place behind them.

COME UNTO THESE YELLOW SANDS, 1847

Huskisson painted this scene in the same year and in the same format as his *Midsummer Night's Fairies* (see page 114). Both pictures were purchased by Samuel Carter Hall, who may perhaps have commissioned this painting as a pendant to the first. The subject is taken from Ariel's song in Act I of *The Tempest*, although Huskisson's immediate source is more likely to have been Dadd's treatment of the theme (see page 20), which was exhibited at the Royal Academy in 1842. The two pictures are very alike, although Huskisson's lyrical colouring is quite distinctive.

Once again he framed the scene in a remarkable *trompe l'oeil* arch. Aside from Dadd, Huskisson also drew inspiration from the work of William Etty (1787–1849) and William Edward Frost (1810–77). Both artists specialized in voluptuous depictions of the female nude, an element that was to feature strongly in early Victorian fairy paintings. In this instance, there are clear borrowings from Frost's *Sabrina* (1845), which in common with Huskisson's pictures was bought and engraved by the *Art Union* publication. These engravings could then be purchased by subscribers. Quite evidently there was a ready and profitable market for the mild eroticism of pictures such as these.

Sir John Everett Millais

Born 1829 Southampton, England

Died 1896

Ferdinand Lured by Ariel, 1849

The subject is drawn from Act I, Scene II of *The Tempest*, where Ferdinand has been shipwrecked on Prospero's island. Ariel, the latter's servant, lures the young man towards his master by whispering the false news that his father has perished in the storm:

> *Full fathom five thy father lies;*
> *Of his bones are corals made;*
> *Those are pearls that were his eyes…*

Ferdinand is baffled by the invisible informant ('Where should this music be? i' the air or the earth?'), but consents to be taken to Prospero, carried by the strange bats that are pictured on the left.

Millais' picture was a bold invention, quite unlike the stagey depictions of Shakespearean fairy subjects that were popular at the time. He took great care to make the human elements appear as realistic as possible. Ferdinand's outfit was taken from Camille Bonnard's *Costumes Historiques*, and the background details were painted with immense precision, right down to the lizard in the corner. In spite of this, he experienced some difficulty in selling the picture. A dealer had reserved it in advance, but withdrew his offer when he saw the finished work. He was disappointed, it appears, with the fairy elements, which lacked the coy eroticism that had become the norm in Victorian fairy scenes.

⚘ A Fairy Song

You spotted snakes, with double tongue,
Thorny hedgehogs, be not seen;
Newts and blind-worms do no wrong,
Come not near our fairy queen.
William Shakespeare,
A Midsummer Night's Dream

Robert Huskisson

Born 1819 England

Died 1861

Titania's Elves Robbing the Squirrel's Nest (detail), *c.* 1854

This may be the painting that Huskisson exhibited at the Royal Academy in 1854, his final appearance at this venue. The title alludes to *A Midsummer Night's Dream*, although this scene does not figure in Shakespeare's play. Indeed, the actions of these fairies are more hostile than the benign creatures who served Titania. Instead they are closer to the fairies of popular tradition, who often had a spiteful streak and were incorrigible theives.. It remains a mystery why Huskisson failed to live up to his early potential, particularly when two of his early fairy paintings were purchased by Samuel Carter Hall. As the editor of the *Art Union* (later the *Art Journal*), Hall was an important figure who certainly had the ability to make an artist's career. Huskisson was clearly in favour for a time as he was invited to produce the frontispiece for a book by Hall's wife in 1848. However, he stopped exhibiting in 1854 and in the following year Hall auctioned off his pictures. By the time of the artist's premature death, the pair had lost contact and Hall later wrote that he "slipped out of the world, no one knew when or how".

John George Naish

Born 1824 London, England

Died 1905

Elves and Fairies: A Midsummer Night's Dream (detail), 1856

Naish trained at the Royal Academy and exhibited there throughout his career. His choice of subject matter varied considerably, but in the 1850s he produced a number of fairy pictures. The most notable examples were *Titania* (1850) and this, his masterpiece, which was shown at the British Institution in 1856.

This does not depict a precise moment in the play, although the fairies and elves (by this stage, the two words were virtually synonymous) do carry out some of the activities mentioned by Shakespeare. On the right, for instance, some fairies attack a caterpillar with tiny spears, recalling Titania's exhortation to her followers to 'kill cankers (i.e. canker-worms or caterpillars) in the musk-rose buds' (Act II, Scene II). On the whole, though, Naish seems more interested in the flowers than the fairies. These are painted with a meticulous attention to detail, very much in the manner of the Pre-Raphaelites. Interestingly they are not Shakespearean flowers, but rather the types of bloom that became popular with Victorian gardeners. The most prominent ones are a fuchsia, a nasturtium and a scarlet geranium. In the 1860s Naish moved to Ilfracombe in Devon, which offered better opportunities to develop his love of nature. For the remainder of his career he worked exclusively on landscapes.

William Bell Scott

Born 1811 Edinburgh, Scotland

Died 1890

Ariel and Caliban (detail), 1865

Scott's picture illustrates a scene from *The Tempest*, where Ariel pours scorn on Caliban and his friends:

> At last I left them,
> In the filthy mantled pool beyond your cell
> There dancing up to th' chins, that foul lake
> O'erstunk their feet…

The theme had a particular interest for Scott, as it provided the subject for one of his brother's (David Scott) finest paintings.

William noted that it was "the most truly poetic production of the painter" and proceeded to explain his interpretation of the characters, who represented "the two poles of human nature; the ascending and descending forces of mind and matter". William adopted this view in his own version of the theme, although his Caliban is far less grotesque than David's.

There has been much discussion about Shakespeare's source for Caliban. Some authorities have noted that the name is almost an anagram of 'cannibal', speculating that it may have been inspired by some of the more lurid travellers' tales about life in the New World. During the latter part of the nineteenth century, the character became associated with Charles Darwin's (1809–82) discoveries about evolution. In several productions Caliban was portrayed as 'the missing link', a creature that lay halfway between ape and man.

Gustave Doré

Born 1832 Strasbourg, France

Died 1883

A Midsummer Night's Dream, c. 1870

Doré's balletic picture serves as a reminder that for much of its history *A Midsummer Night's Dream* was performed as a spectacle of music and dance, rather than a traditional play. Generations of directors found it virtually impossible to stage and made savage cuts to the text. It was performed only once during the Restoration period, when Pepys praised the dancing but condemned the rest as "the most insipid ridiculous play that I ever saw in my life". In his version, David Garrick (1717–79) removed all but 600 lines of the original text, basing the performance around the antics of the fairies and the lovers.

A greater sense of balance was restored by Madame Lucia Vestris. In her 1840 production she restored most of Shakespeare's text, although opera and ballet still took precedence over drama. In particular, during the supernatural scenes, the stage was filled with crowds of female fairies wearing costumes made of white gauze. This became a feature of many productions throughout the nineteenth century and clearly provided the inspiration for Doré's picture. In her production Vestris actually took the part of Oberon herself. This started a trend for both the fairy rulers to be played by women. Traditionally Oberon was a contralto, while Titania was a soprano.

JOHN SIMMONS

BORN 1823 Bristol, England

DIED 1876

There Sleeps Titania (detail), 1872

Simmons' title refers to a line from Act II of *A Midsummer Night's Dream*: 'There sleeps Titania sometime of the night'. This episode proved particularly appealing to Victorian artists: Dadd and Huskisson both painted precisely the same scene (see pages 17 and 114). Simmons' version has more in common with the latter, most notably in the theatrical way that Titania is placed under a spotlight.

Simmons has emphasized the erotic charms of the fairy queen. This has raised a few modern critics' eyebrows, but the artist's contemporaries were less concerned. His career coincided with the passing of the Obscene Publications Act in 1857. This had little real impact on painters, although some shopkeepers were instructed to remove prints of nude pictures from their windows. From the outset, the Act was mainly directed against nude photographs. Here the usual defence was that they were art studies, designed for painters who were too poor to afford a live model. Simmons' work was exempt from any such problems – his nudes were acceptable partly because they were fairies, but even more so because they were illustrations of Shakespeare. In their attempts to promote a national British school, the authorities did their utmost to encourage painters to tackle themes from British literature and history.

Titania (detail)

When the fashion for fairy paintings was at its peak, there was a tendency for artists to cram their canvases full of colourful, anecdotal details of the little people. Simmons cut against this trend. Instead, he usually focused on a single, female fairy, depicting her in a variety of semi-erotic poses. As a result, his paintings are sometimes now described as Victorian pin-ups. Simmons' use of nudity was rarely censured at the time, although there were critics who opposed the general increase in subjects of this kind. The most vocal of these was John Horsley, the Treasurer of the Royal Academy, who believed that nudes should be banned from public exhibition on the grounds of morality. He became closely involved in the so-called 'British Matron' controversy of 1885, when a letter to *The Times*, signed anonymously by a British Matron (although many believed that it was actually Horsley), sparked off a national debate on the topic. Ultimately, however, Horsley was swimming against the tide. The most respectable art of the day, Classical paintings produced by the leading academicians, relied heavily on the nude. In addition, it had the royal seal of approval. Queen Victoria purchased several paintings of nudes as birthday presents for Prince Albert and went out of her way to praise Landseer's depiction of Lady Godiva.

The Sleep of Titania (detail)

This nocturnal scene is based very loosely on *A Midsummer Night's Dream*. Queen Titania lies sleeping in the woods, and when she awakens she will fall in love with Bottom. The theme of sleeping and dreams was highly popular during the Romantic era, and not just with fairy painters. Artists increasingly regarded dreams as the gateway to the imagination. Henry Fuseli (1741–1825) is said to have consumed a plate of raw beef just before retiring in the hope that it would bring him more impressive dreams. The nude also became a more common subject in nineteenth-century Britain.

To some extent this was a patriotic move designed to give the country a greater standing within the international art world. Britain had been slow to develop a national school or tradition, although William Hogarth (1697–1764) had begun the campaign to establish one, complaining at the way that major commissions were automatically given to foreign artists. The depiction of the nude formed an important part of this process. Ever since the Renaissance, the study of the human figure had been the cornerstone of academic training. The absence of a British tradition in this field was a cause for concern.

Hermia and Lysander

Hermia and Lysander are the two young lovers who elope from Athens after their romance meets with parental disapproval. They spend the night in the woods, where life becomes more complicated after Puck places the magical juice in Lysander's eye, causing him to fall for Helena. Simmons' painting depicts the interlude before Puck's interference, when the couple are so blinded by love that they do not notice the swarms of tiny fairies who are busily engaged all around them. It is no accident that most of the action of A Midsummer Night's Dream takes place in a wood. In Tudor times 'wood' was an everyday term for 'mad', and Shakespeare used this to punning effect throughout the course of the play. Thus Demetrius describes himself as 'wood (i.e. frantic) within this wood/Because I cannot meet my Hermia.' (Act II, Scene I, 192–3). The wooing of the lovers offered scope for further puns – Helena and Hermia are wooed within a wood. The irrational overtones of a wood made it a suitable environment for fairies. Moonlight, too, had similar associations. It was a symbol of change and inconstancy, while lunacy gained its name from the belief that madness was brought on by the Moon.

A Fairy Verse

Fetch me that flower;
The herb I show'd thee once:
The juice of it on sleeping eyelids laid
Will make a man or woman madly dote
Upon the next live creature that it sees.

William Shakespeare,
A Midsummer Night's Dream

Gustave Doré

Born 1832 Strasbourg, France

Died 1883

The Fairies: A Scene Drawn from Shakespeare, 1873

Despite the title, Doré's picture is a very loose adaptation from *A Midsummer Night's Dream*. Oberon and Titania have been reconciled and now preside over the fairy revels. The tiny creatures flock to their leaders from all quarters and can even be seen silhouetted against the Moon. Oberon's somewhat effeminate appearance can be explained by the fact that the part was often played by a woman. The differences in scale are specified in Shakespeare's play. Titania is large enough to cradle Bottom's head in her lap, while her attendants are noted for their minute stature.

Gustave Doré was a hugely versatile artist, who is probably better remembered now as a book illustrator rather than a painter. He had a gift for depicting the fantastic, as his illustrations for Dante's (1265–1321) *Inferno* (c. 1314) and Samuel Taylor Coleridge's (1772–1834) *Rime of the Ancient Mariner* (1798) confirm. However, when the occasion arose, he could also be grimly realistic. His scenes of London's slums, for example, were much admired by Van Gogh (1853–90). Indeed, his work was highly popular in England, and from 1868 to 1892 there was a Doré gallery in New Bond Street.

Flourished 1885–91

Midsummer Fairies

Dell painted a series of fairy pictures in the 1880s mostly following a set pattern. Her subjects were diminutive fairies, usually female, disporting themselves in a silvan retreat. Their tiny size is emphasized by the enormous blooms and insects that surround them. The fairies appear to give off their own light, with the centre of the composition resembling the warm glow of a spotlight. Here, for example, the huge yellow rose is clearly lit from below, rather than above. At first glance the ambiguity of the lighting may disguise the fact that the background is a starry night sky, which is just visible through the fretwork of leaves and flowers.

    Midsummer Fairies is set within a proscenium arch. This, together with the dramatic lighting, lends the picture a theatrical air, which is shared by so many other fairy paintings. The link with the stage is further strengthened by the picture's title. Dell produced a number of scenes, such as *Titania's Bower*, that refer to *A Midsummer Night's Dream* without actually depicting a specific episode from it. In this instance it is possible that the sleeping figure in the foreground, who is isolated from the rest of the group, is meant to represent Titania.

Etheline E. Dell

Sir Hubert Von Herkomer

Born 1849 Waal, Bavaria

Died 1914

Bottom Asleep, 1891

Shakespeare is thought to have had two sources in mind when creating the character of Bottom. Firstly there was the famous legend of King Midas, who was given the ears of an ass after offending Apollo. In addition there was the tale of Apuleius in *The Golden Ass*, in which the narrator persuades his mistress to steal a jar of ointment from a witch in the hope that it will transform him into a bird. Instead, to his dismay, he finds himself turned into an ass. During this transformation period, however, a friendly maid offers to "finely combe thy maine" and "tye up thy rugged tayle", which may have given the playwright the idea for Titania's flirtation.

Herkomer became best known as a portraitist, although he worked successfully in several different fields. His most celebrated painting was *The Last Muster – Sunday at the Royal Hospital, Chelsea*, a patriotic celebration of British military pride. Throughout his life he was passionate about the stage, running his own private theatre at Bushey in Hertfordshire. He also set up an art school there in 1883, where William Nicholson (1872–1949) became one of his pupils.

Charles Wilhelm

Born 1858 England

Died 1925

The Bindweed Fairy, costume design

Wilhelm created this costume design for R. Courtneidge's production of *A Midsummer Night's Dream* at the Princes Theatre in Manchester. Bindweed is not a named member of Shakespeare's cast, but by the end of the nineteenth century the link between flowers and fairies had become so ingrained that it was natural for Wilhelm to use different plants as a linking theme for Titania's attendants. Wilhelm himself was one of the most prolific costume designers in the Edwardian era. He is remembered in particular for his work on pantomimes, and he also produced the costumes for one of the earliest stagings of *Peter Pan*.

Shakespeare made great play of the diminutive size of his fairies, so it is likely that he used child actors for these parts. Over the years directors have come up with some highly imaginative variations on this theme. During the Romantic era they were usually portrayed as ballet dancers dressed in white gauze, whether adult women or children. In Harley Granville-Barker's (1877–1946) revolutionary 1914 production, however, they were covered in gold paint, resembling Indian deities. In 1954 George Devine (1910–65) opted for feathered, bird-like costumes, while in Peter Brook's (b. 1925) startling version of 1970 the fairies were interpreted as adult, male circus performers.

Sophie Anderson

Born 1823 Paris, France

Died 1903

Thus Your Fairy's Made of Most Beautiful Things

The title of this work refers to a verse by Charles Ede:

> *Take the fair face of woman,*
> *and gently suspending.*
> *With butterflies, flowers and*
> *jewels attending,*
> *Thus your fairy is made of*
> *most beautiful things.*

Anderson specialized in paintings of children, with a particular preference for young girls. A few of these have fairy accessories, although it is unclear whether they were meant to represent fairies or were simply girls in fairy costume. Either way this is certainly the finest of her fairy pictures. It was exhibited at the Royal Society of British Artists in 1869.

Anderson was born in France, the daughter of a French architect and an English mother. After the 1848 Revolution the family fled to the United States, residing mainly in Pittsburgh and Cincinnati. While there she forged a successful career as a portraitist, which she cemented after moving to England in 1854. She married an English artist, Walter Anderson.

Walter Crane

Born 1845 Liverpool, England

Died 1915

Costumes for Elves and Fairy Painters, 1899

By the later stages of the nineteenth century, fairies were so much in vogue that they were used to satirize the major institutions of the day. Even Queen Victoria was affectionately known as 'the Faery' by her prime minister. These costumes were designed for *The Snowman*, a pantomime that was staged at the Lyceum Theatre in December 1899. Several members of the Art Workers' Guild were involved in the show, in which they poked fun at the current art scene. The figure on the left, holding the palette and the sketching board, is one of the fairy painters. On the right his model represents Aestheticism, a literary and artistic movement

that was epitomized by the dandyish figures of Oscar Wilde (1854–1900) and James McNeill Whistler (1834–1903). The lily in her left hand and the peacock motif on her dress were the favourite emblems of the group, while the mirror in her right hand echoed the general public's belief that the Aesthetes were highly narcissistic. The Art Workers' Guild had been formed in 1884 as a means of bringing about closer co-operation between the various branches of the decorative arts. This was parodied in the finale of *The Snowman*, when fairy architects jostled with fairy potters, weavers and carpenters.

Walter Jenks Morgan

Born 1847 Bilston, England

Died 1924

'Where rural fays and fairies dwell'

Morgan took the title of his painting from a poem by William
Shenstone (1714–63):

> Here, in cool grot and mossy cell,
> Where rural fays and fairies dwell;
> Though rarely seen by mortal eye…

Shenstone was a landscape gardener as well as a poet, and
he combined these vocations in a collection of verses entitled
Inscriptions (1865). These lines were conceived as poems that might
be found scattered around his estate at Leasowes, near Halesowen,
inscribed on such items as urns, obelisks and seats. Shenstone's
description of the fairy revels is very conventional, even down to
the warning contained in the final lines:

> And tread with awe these favour'd bowers,
> Nor wound the shrubs, nor bruise the flowers;
> So may your path with sweets abound;
> So may your couch with rest be crown'd!
> But harm betide the wayward swain,
> Who dares our hallow'd haunts profane!

Walter Morgan was trained at the Birmingham School of Art.
After serving an apprenticeship with a lithographer, he made his name
as an illustrator, contributing regularly to the *Graphic* and the *Illustrated
London News*. He became president of the Midlands Art Club and the
Birmingham Art Circle.

Jean and Ron Henry

Ron Henry Born 1936 London England

Jean Henry Born 1943 London England

Bottom of the Garden (detail), 1988

This charming, modern slant on the fairy world takes its name from 'The Fairies' by Rose Fyleman (1877–1957):

There are fairies at the bottom of our garden!
It's not so very, very far away:
You pass the gardener's shed and you just keep straight ahead –
I do so hope they've really come to stay.
There's a little wood, with moss in it and beetles,
And a little stream that quietly runs through;
You wouldn't think they'd dare to come merry –
making there – Well they do.

Fyleman's poem was published in *Punch* in 1917 at the height of the First World War. It proved an instant hit with the public and she became a regular contributor to the magazine. In the following year her first collection of verse, *Fairies and Chimneys*, went into print. The poem may well have inspired Elsie Wright and Frances Griffiths to produce their fairy photographs in Cottingley Glen. Their chosen location corresponds quite closely to Fyleman's description and Elsie admitted that she knew the poem.

Brian Froud

Born 1947 Winchester, England

Gwenhwyfar, 1993

Gwenhwyfar is one of the good fairies in Froud's bestselling book, *Good Faeries, Bad Faeries* (1998). In the text he defines her as the White Shadow, an ethereal spirit dancing under the moonlight to the tune of a fairy piper. In her wake she leaves a trail of glowing, star-shaped flowers, which grow from her footsteps. As she dances her eyes are closed and she dreams that she is far away, drifting in an unknown galaxy of stars. Froud also links Gwenhwyfar with the White Ladies, "luminous faery creatures who dance by the light of the moon". This term has been used to describe both ghosts and fairies. It has a particular relevance to Gwenhwyfar, as the literal meaning of her name is 'white phantom'. The White Ladies could be benevolent, although some were distinctly dangerous. The White Lady of Lough Gur, for example, claimed a human life every seven years.

Gwenhwyfar is a Welsh variant of Guinevere, a name that is inevitably associated with the adulterous wife of King Arthur. It has also been seen as the counterpart of the Irish name Finnabair, which is traditionally linked with the beautiful daughter of Maeve, the goddess of war.

George Cruikshank

Born 1792 London, England

Died 1878

Fairyland Scenes

There are many pictures showing fairies at war with their neighbours. In Cruikshank's piece of knockabout fun, however, the roles are reversed. Normally the fairies have the upper hand, but here the insects take their revenge, pinching and stinging their diminutive foes. The colourful gnomes or dwarfs are fine comic creations, but they clearly stem from the world of children's literature rather than the darker realms of traditional folklore.

Fairies played a relatively minor role in Cruikshank's career. He started out as a political caricaturist, lampooning the follies of Napoleon and the Prince Regent. Later on he became better known as a social commentator. In particular he was known for his campaigning cartoons on behalf of the Temperance movement, which became a near obsession after the 1840s. Cruikshank was also a prolific book illustrator. He produced his most celebrated work for Charles Dickens (1812–70) while, in terms of fairy material, he is chiefly associated with the first English edition of *German Popular Stories* (1823–26) by the Brothers Grimm.

Herbert Cole

BORN 1867 London, England

DIED 1930

Father Time (detail), 1906

This illustration was produced by Herbert Cole for *Fairy-Gold: A Book of Classic English Fairy Tales* (1906) by Ernest Rhys (1859–1946). Cole was a prolific illustrator of magazines and children's books. He is probably best remembered for his work on the 1900 edition of Gulliver's Travels and the 1903 version of *The Ingoldsby Legends*. Ernest Rhys was a distinguished writer, who was born in London but brought up in Carmarthen. He worked for a time in the coal industry before turning to literature. In 1885 he moved to London, where he became a founder member of the Rhymers' Club, a group of poets who met in the Cheshire Cheese in Fleet Street. His most lasting achievement was as the founding editor of the Everyman's Library series of affordable classics.

Folk beliefs about the fairies' attitude to time and death are very varied. Some sources argued that fairies could not fear death, since they themselves were actually the spirits of the dead who had not been baptized. Others believed that they did not actually die, but gradually dwindled away, shrinking a little every time they used their shape-shifting skills.

❧ A Fairy Rhyme
Couldst thou, Great Fairy, give to me
The instant's wish, that I might see
Of all the earth's that one dear sight
Known only in a dream's delight ...
Harriet Prescott Spofford, 'The Pines'

Warwick Goble

BORN 1862 London, England

DIED 1943

'The fairies came flying in at the window...' (detail), 1909

This is one of Goble's illustrations for the 1909 edition of Charles Kingsley's (1819–75) masterpiece, *The Water Babies, A Fairy Tale for a Land-Baby*. It shows the fairies fitting a new pair of wings to a young girl. Kingsley's story demonstrates the way that children's literature altered fairy traditions. Tom, the orphaned chimney sweep, can only find happiness after he has died and been transformed into a water baby. This was a reversal of the older folk tales, where fairies were feared for their practice of stealing children away from their rightful family. Kingsley's book also had a campaigning edge to it: significantly, the law on the use of children as chimney sweeps was changed within a year of its original date of publication (1863). Indeed, the author had been inspired to write The Water Babies after reading a damning government report about the increased use of 'climbing-boys' in the trade. By profession Kingsley was a clergyman, but he was probably better known to his contemporaries as a social reformer. He helped run a periodical called Politics for the People, and courted controversy by announcing, "What is the use of preaching about Heaven to hungry paupers?".

John McKirdy Duncan

Born 1866 Scotland

Died 1945

Yorinda and Yoringel in the Witch's Wood, 1909

The subject is taken from one of Grimm's fairy tales. The two lovers, Jorinda and Joringel, are wandering through a wood when they fall foul of an evil witch. She turns Jorinda into a nightingale and then imprisons her in her castle, where she has 7,000 other maidens trapped in the form of birds. Joringel is desperate to free his beloved and return her to her original state. He eventually achieves this, with the aid of a magic flower. Duncan's painting is a very loose adaptation of the start of the story. The two are so in love that they barely notice the circle of good fairies, who dance around them. These fairies bring light to the forest, but cannot protect the lovers from the forces of darkness that await them. A witch can take the form of a screeching owl or cat, but is represented here by the old woman, sitting cross-legged on the far left. The fire is for roasting the wild animals and birds, which are lured into the reaches of her power.

Grimm's fairy tales were first published in English as *German Popular Stories* in 1824. Duncan painted a number of fairy pictures, mostly with Celtic overtones. He entered into the spirit of his subject matter, claiming that he heard fairy music while he worked.

Charles James Folkard

Born 1878 England

Died 1963

Fairy with Wings

Fairies were never the same after *Peter Pan*. Once the bond between children and fairies was firmly established, the darker elements of fairyland were gradually excluded. Even in the drawings of Arthur Rackham, who had a definite taste for the grotesque, the fairies were generally the least threatening elements. On top of this, artists were well aware of the growing commercial opportunities. Their illustrations did not just appear in books; they were also available on posters, cards, prints and calendars, and this was a further incentive for steering clear of any controversy.

The glorious colouring of this fairy may owe a debt to the exotic style of Edmund Dulac. Folkard himself was a prolific illustrator and cartoonist. He illustrated many of the classic children's books, among them *Mother Goose Nursery Rhymes*, *Old Mother Hubbard*, *The Arabian Nights* and many more.

Edmund Dulac

Born 1882 Toulouse, France

Died 1953

'She found herself face to face with a stately and beautiful lady...' (detail), 1910

This is Dulac's illustration for the story of *Beauty and the Beast* which appeared in the 1910 edition of *The Sleeping Beauty and other Fairy Tales* by Sir Arthur Quiller-Couch (1863–1944). In the story the fairy appears to Beauty, urging her to go and stay at the Beast's palace so that her father can be freed. She also appears at the close of the tale, when Beauty's unselfish virtue is rewarded. Dulac was a stage designer, among other things, and there is little doubt that his experience in that field was relevant here. *Beauty and the Beast* evolved from a folk tale, but in the nineteenth century it was also performed as a pantomime. With her rich apparel and her wand, this figure is based on a traditional fairy godmother, a role that might be described as the secular equivalent of a guardian angel. Dulac was Rackham's only serious rival during the Edwardian period. Both men excelled at producing illustrations for the lavish, gift editions of classic stories. Ostensibly these books were designed for children, although they doubtless appealed even more to adults.

Frederick George Cotman

Born 1850 England

Died 1920

Spellbound (detail), 1912

Few people will have difficulty in recognizing this scene as a key episode from the story of *Sleeping Beauty*. A wicked fairy has decreed that the princess will fall into a deep sleep, if she pricks her finger on a spindle. In a bid to prevent this, the king has prohibited the use of these machines, but his daughter eventually comes across one hidden away in a dusty old attic. As she pricks her finger the spell comes into force. The story dates back to the fourteenth century, although the best-known version was by Charles Perrault (1628–1703) and was translated into English in 1729. Cotman took the unusual step of portraying the subject in modern dress, rather than in the customary medieval setting.

Frederick Cotman belonged to a distinguished East Anglian family of artists. He was the nephew of John Sell Cotman (1782–1842), a famous landscape painter who became one of the leading lights of the Norwich School. Frederick entered the Royal Academy in 1868 and began showing his work there in 1871. He won his first award for a history painting, *The Death of Eucles* (1873), but soon followed a similar path to his uncle by specializing in landscapes. *Spellbound* was a very rare excursion into the realms of fantasy.

❧ A Fairy Song
Help, as if from faery power,
Dewy night o'ershades the ground;
Turn the swift wheel round and round!
William Wordsworth,
'Song for the Spinning Wheel'

Warwick Goble

Born 1862 London, England

Died 1943

Fairies Around a Baby's Cot (detail), 1920

This illustration is one of the 16 plates that Goble designed for *The Book of Fairy Poetry* (1920), an anthology edited by Dora Owen. Goble illustrated a number of books in the 1890s, most notably *The War of the Worlds* (1898) by H. G. Wells (1866–1946), but he did not make his mark in children's literature until the following decade. In the early Edwardian period the success of Rackham and Dulac created a vogue for lavishly illustrated children's classics, prompting publishers to seek out similar artists. Goble's work on *The Water Babies* helped to establish him in this field. He never reached the dizzying heights of Rackham or Dulac, but his interest in Japanese art brought him a lucrative series of commissions on Asian projects. Indeed, he probably produced his best work for *Green Willow and Other Japanese Fairy Tales* (1910).

Joyce Dennys

Born 1893 England

Died 1991

Oh Grown-Ups Cannot Understand

This is an illustration of a well-known verse by the poet and lecturer, Alfred Noyes (1880–1958):

> *Oh grown-ups cannot understand*
> *and grown-ups never will*
> *How short the way to fairyland*
> *Across the purple hill.*

Noyes' sentiments underline the gradual shift in relationships between fairies and children. In their early appearances in literature, fairies were more likely to communicate with adults than children. If anything the child tended to be a victim, like the stolen Indian boy in *A Midsummer Night's Dream*. During the late Victorian and Edwardian period, however, when fairies were increasingly relegated to the nursery, this trend was reversed. Children became the confidants of fairies, while adults were ruthlessly

excluded. This was most famously the case in *Peter Pan*, where
Wendy's mother mused nostalgically on her own childhood
adventures with the boy, which could never be repeated after she
had grown up. In a similar fashion the myth about stolen babies
was significantly altered: the fairies now became rescuers, only
taking children that were unwanted or unloved. This was the
theme of Rudyard Kipling's (1865–1936) tale, *Cold Iron*.
Dennys was a prolific illustrator and
author, best remembered perhaps
for *Henrietta's War: News
from the Home Front,
1939–1942*, a humorous
account of life in
wartime Devon.

Folklore & Myths

The cute faces and charming frolics of the fairies that appear in children's storybooks are a far cry from the strange race of creatures, which has featured for centuries in folk traditions. The myths surrounding them stretch back to ancient times and differ greatly, from place to place. Their origins, for example, have been explained in many diverse ways. For some people, they are fallen angels, while others see them as gods who have lost their powers. Then again, they may be the ghosts of the dead or, alternatively, the spirits who protect our vanished ancestors.

There are stories both of good fairies and bad fairies. Good fairies, for instance, may help with housework or cleaning, if they are rewarded with a bowl of milk or a morsel of bread. Most superstitions, however, relate to bad fairies. If a mortal spies on fairy activities or comes into contact with them, whether by accident or not, there is usually a price to be paid. They may be spirited away to fairyland, never to return, or else cursed with some terrible affliction, such as blindness or insanity.

George Cruikshank

Born 1792 London, England

Died 1878

A Fairy Gathering

In this entertaining scene, Cruikshank's impish fairies produce a highly comical dance for their distinguished guests. Even so the picture has a sinister edge. The broken eggshell on the right has presumably been violated by the dancers. This may explain the curious, bird-like creature on the left, who peers down angrily at the proceedings.

There have been many reported sightings of fairy dances, one of the earliest coming from the antiquarian John Aubrey (1626–97), who related the experience of his local curate: "he sawe an innumerable quantitie of very small people, dancing rounde and rounde… making all maner of small odd noyses". The curate tried to run away, but found that he could not move, "being, as he supposes, kept there in a kind of enchantment". At length when the fairies spotted him, "they surrounded him on all sides… and pinched him all over, and made a sorte of quick humming noyse… ". Perhaps he escaped lightly, for W. B. Yeats (1865–1939) told an alarming tale of a woman who was stolen away in her youth. When she returned seven years later, she had no toes, having danced them off in fairyland.

Amelia Jane Murray (Lady Oswald)

Born 1800 Port-e-Chee, Isle of Man

Died 1896

A Fairy Standing on a Moth While Being Chased by a Butterfly

Amelia Murray was one of the first artists to ignore the more threatening elements of fairy folklore, portraying the creatures as dainty and diminutive. She developed an interest in the subject at an early age, largely because of her background. She was born on the Isle of Man, in an area steeped in ancient, Celtic traditions (her birthplace was said to mean 'fairy music' in Gaelic). From childhood these tales were a source of endless fascination to her, inspiring her to begin painting fairies from the 1820s.

From her precisely drawn studies of flowers and insects, it is clear that Murray also took an interest in contemporary books and periodicals on natural history. These were not as far removed from fairy matters as might be imagined. In a bid to popularize their subject, authors would sometimes introduce fantasy elements. In *Fairy Frisket, Or Peeps at the Insect Folk*, a children's guide to the insect world, the narrators are two fairies. Similarly in *Episodes of Insect Life* (1849–51), a more adult book on the same subject, there are detailed illustrations of spiders and beetles, accompanied by whimsical little fairies dressed in tiny suits of armour.

Daniel Maclise

BORN 1806 Cork, Ireland

DIED 1870

The Faun and the Fairies (detail), c. 1834

Maclise produced this remarkable painting for the novelist, Edward Bulwer Lytton (1803–73), calling it *Pan and the Dancing Fairies*. The latter had it engraved and used it as an illustration in one of his works, *The Pilgrims of the Rhine* (1834), a curious book combining German folklore, travel writing and romance. More specifically he used it for a story entitled *The Complaint of the Last Faun*, which included a scene based on the painting. This described how the sylvan figure was persuaded to play his pipes, so that the fairies could begin their swirling dance. In the centre meanwhile, three hideous goblins loiter inside a cave. After the publication of the book the name of the picture was changed.

Although he forged his reputation as a history painter, Maclise also made a significant contribution to the development of the fairy picture. He exerted a powerful influence on several of the leading figures in this field, most notably Dadd and Paton. His work also found favour at the highest level. In 1844 Queen Victoria purchased *Undine*, Maclise's finest fairy painting, as a birthday present for Prince Albert.

❧ A Fairy Verse
The maidens danced about it morn and noon,
And learnèd bards of it their ditties made;
The nimble fairies by the pale-faced moon
Water'd the root and kiss'd her pretty shade.
William Browne, of Tavistock, 'The Rose'

Robert Alexander Hillingford

Born 1825 Surrey, England

Died 1904

The Fairy Dance

By the mid-Victorian period, fairy subjects had become so popular that they were attracting painters from a variety of different fields. Hillingford typifies this trend. The son of an officer, he enjoyed a distinguished career as a military artist. He worked initially in Germany, studying at the Academy Schools in Düsseldorf and becoming a leading member of the German Artists Club. After this, he lived in Italy for 16 years, before finally settling in London in 1864. There, he rapidly established a reputation in the conventional art world, exhibiting regularly at the Royal Academy.

In addition to his military pictures, Hillingford produced historical and Shakespearean themes. *The Fairy Dance* was painted in a similar vein. Unlike most contemporary versions of the theme, it is not reminiscent of the ballet or the theatre. Instead, the picture has an eerie quality. The women seem to be performing a ritual or conjuring up a spell, rather than simply dancing and, with their sturdy figures, they are more akin to the witches in *Macbeth*, hovering 'through the foul and filthy air', than to ethereal fairies.

Charles Altamont Doyle

BORN 1832 London, England

DIED 1893

A Band of Fairies

This is an unusually tranquil scene for Doyle – his paintings are normally crowded with humorous details. The treatment of a fairy dance was equally untypical. Fairies were seen as a secretive people; they preferred to seek their entertainments in sheltered places, forest glades, flowery dells and leafy river banks rather than the open countryside. The sweeping panorama betrays the influence of the Romantic movement. During this period, landscape artists often sought out rugged, spectacular scenery that created a strong impression on the senses. Doyle spent most of his career in Scotland and thus had ample opportunity to explore the Highlands. Even so, the need to portray the fairy figures on a visible scale created an obvious problem, lessening the impact of the distant peaks.

Charles Doyle came from an artistic family. He was the son of John Doyle (1797–1868), who enjoyed a successful career as a political caricaturist; his elder brother was Richard Doyle (1824–83), who was an illustrator as well as a purveyor of fairy subjects; but his most famous relative was his son, Sir Arthur Conan Doyle (1859–1930), the creator of Sherlock Holmes. Conan Doyle led the defence of the Cottingley fairy photographs. This in turn begs the question whether Charles also believed in fairies.

✤ A Fairy Rhyme

Then come, you fairies, dance with me a round;
Melt her hard heart with your melodious sound.
In vain are all the charms I can devise;
She hath an art to break them with her eyes.

Thomas Campion,
'Thrice Toss These Oaken Ashes in the Air'

A Dance Around the Moon

Doyle had a whimsical approach to fairy painting. His tiny characters are usually humorous, performing balancing acts with flowers and cheating at cards, although they occasionally have a flavour of something more sinister. So it is in this painting. The scene resembles a mad scramble, rather than a dance. Parts of it would not look out of place in a Keystone Cops routine. Jockeys, huntsmen, lawyers and police are caught up in a chase, alongside characters from fairy tales and mischievous sprites. In the centre there is a quirky depiction of a nightmare, complete with an impish incubus. A woman's hair has

been transformed into the mare's tail, however, and she is dragged along painfully in its wake.

Doyle's fragile health may have given an edge to his work. In the 1880s he was committed to the Montrose Royal Lunatic Asylum suffering from a combination of epilepsy and alcoholism. With typical gallows humour, he immediately dubbed the place 'Sunnyside'. Doyle continued to paint in these later years, giving rise to obvious comparisons with Dadd. In common with the latter, Doyle managed to convey an irrational concoction of images with dream-like clarity.

Sir Edward Coley Burne-Jones

Born 1833 Birmingham, England

Died 1898

Hill Fairies (detail), c. 1881

The painting now known as *Hill Fairies* was originally intended to
be part of a triptych. Burne-Jones designed it as one of the side panels
for his work *Arthur in Avalon*, a major project commissioned by the
Earl of Carlisle. The huge, central panel, measuring more than 20 ft
(6 m), was to show the sleeping warrior in his otherworldly resting
place. According to legend he was destined to remain there until the
nation needed him again, when a terrific noise would rouse him from
his slumbers. The side panels, meanwhile, showed the 'fairies' waiting
for this moment. Burne-Jones conceived these creatures as the spirits
of the hills. More specifically they were the echoes that dwelt in the
fissures between the rocks, ready to repeat the trumpet blare that
would one day wake the king from his long sleep.

Significantly, this picture bears no resemblance to the standard
type of Victorian fairy painting, which Burne-Jones regarded as a
minor, specialist branch of the art scene. Instead, his inspiration
stemmed from the Italian Renaissance, and his figures were closer
to Classical nymphs than to the traditional idea of fairies. As such
they did not blend easily with the Arthurian theme, so at an early
stage Burne-Jones decided to dispense with the side panels. They
were eventually sold off separately.

Henry Meynell Rheam

Born 1859 Birkenhead, England

Died 1920

The Fairy Wood (detail), 1903

Rheam painted a series of paintings in a rich, Pre-Raphaelite vein, showing beautiful young women lost in the woods. Here, a high-born maiden is led away from the safety of the open country. Unwarily she is treading on a bluebell patch where fairy enchantments are at their strongest. Bluebell woods are also the haunts of the notorious oak men, with their red toadstool caps. Although most fairy painters looked to Shakespeare as a source, they also associated fairies with the Middle Ages. In particular they linked the period with Morgan le Fay, the fairy sister of King Arthur, who was known for her skills as a sorceress.

Rheam was born in Birkenhead, but pursued his studies in London and Paris. After his return he made his name as a watercolourist. He lived for a time in Polperro, but spent most of his life in Newlyn, a Cornish fishing port. This may seem surprising since his work could hardly have been more different from that of the Newlyn School, the local artists' colony. Its leader, Stanhope Forbes (1857–1947), insisted that Rheam was persuaded to join them in Newlyn because of his skill as a cricketer, so that he could play for their team against the rival colony at St Ives.

Edward Robert Hughes

BORN 1849 London, England

Died 1914

Midsummer Eve (detail), 1908

During the later stages of the nineteenth century, a growing number of artists showed humans coming into contact with fairies. These encounters were usually friendly, unlike the earlier examples in folk tales or fairy literature where the humans were invariably punished for intruding on the privacy of the tiny creatures. This painting has some affinities with *The Introduction* by Eleanor Fortescue Brickdale (1871–1945), although Hughes's picture is far more atmospheric. This is largely due to the ambiguity, which arises from the uncertain link between the woman and the fairies. At first glance she appears to be human, but it is quite possible that she is meant to be some form of wood nymph. Her bare feet confirm that she is no casual passer-by, while the rapturous welcome she receives within the fairy ring is most uncharacteristic. Moreover, the flowers that adorn her dress and hair offer the suggestion that she may herself be a woodland creature. Most telling of all is the pipe that dangles from her side. From this it can be deduced that the girl has drawn the fairies to her by playing their magical music on her instrument. As such she is a forerunner of *The Piper of Dreams* (see page 161).

A Fairy Song

And when I join the fairy band,
Lightly tripping hand in hand,
By the moonlight's quivering beam,
In concert with the dashing stream;
Then my music leads the dance ....

Felicia Dorothea Browne-Hemans,
'Fairy Song'

Charles Sims

Born 1873 London, England

Died 1928

'...and the fairies ran away with their clothes' (detail)

There are many tales of fairies using their powers in order to steal from humans. The most serious cases involved babies. Reports of these date back to the Middle Ages, when they were recorded in the chronicles of Ralph of Coggeshall (*c.* 1210). The principal targets were unchristened infants, who lacked the protection of the Church. When the child was stolen a changeling was left in its place, usually an ancient withered fairy. In the past children that were born with a handicap were sometimes deemed to be changelings.

On a lighter note, fairies were notorious for stealing food. Occasionally they would take the entire article, but more often they would extract the goodness from the food, its 'foison', and leave behind a stale husk. On a grander scale they sometimes lured cows away from the fold so that they could steal their milk. Clothes were a less obvious target, although the fairies would steal anything if a human had offended them in some way. By the same token, those who found favour with the little people were rewarded. When a hunchback called Lusmore pleased them with a song they took away his hump and gave him a brand new suit of clothes.

Estella Louisa Michaela Canziani

Born 1887 Italy

Died 1964

The Piper of Dreams, 1914

This is one of the last great fairy paintings. A boy leans against a tree wearing a peacock feather in his hat, a traditional symbol of immortality. He is playing a magical strain of fairy music, which draws the woodland creatures to his side. A robin perches on his shoe, a squirrel approaches on the right, while around his head diaphanous fairies swoop and swirl.

Canziani painted this memorable scene when she was staying with the classical scholar, Gilbert Murray. His son was the model for the piper, while the woods behind their cottage provided the setting. The picture was exhibited at the Royal Academy in 1915 where it was sold on Private View Day. The reproduction rights were acquired by the Medici Society and the picture became an international bestseller. More than a quarter of a million prints of it were sold within a year. In many cases these were hung in the nursery, but thousands were also sent to soldiers in the trenches. Many of them wrote to the artist expressing their appreciation. For them the tranquil, fairyland scene was a nostalgic reminder of the world they had left behind, a world that they feared might not survive.

Grace Jones

Born unknown

Died unknown

The Fairy Dance, c. 1920

By the early years of the twentieth century, many of the old superstitions about fairies had all but died away. Few Victorian artists would have envisaged a child enjoying such a happy scene as is depicted. Instead they would have feared for her safety, given the fairies' reputation for stealing pretty, young children. They would have been equally horrified at the way the girl is sitting inside the ring. This, too, was fraught with danger. Any mortal who stepped inside a fairy ring was liable to come under their power. They might force their victim to join the dance, refusing to release them for months on end. Worse still, they might carry them away to fairyland. Some people never returned from that magical place, while others only came back after many years had passed. In addition they were unlikely to survive such a journey and some crumbled to dust the moment they returned to the real world, while others just slowly pined away.

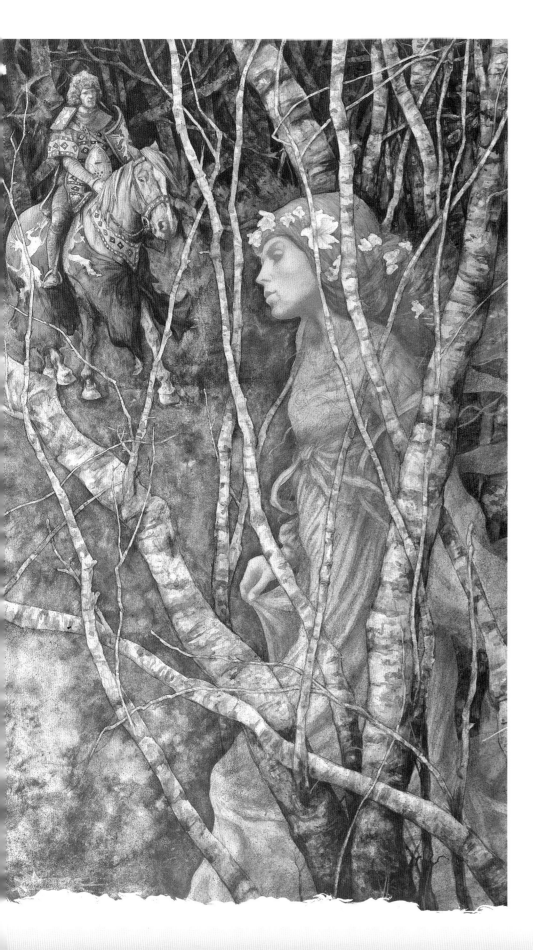

Brian Froud

BORN 1947 Winchester, England

The Elfin Maid, 1976

Female fairies were often seen as great seductresses, captivating men with their beauty, but romances between mortals and fairies were perilous affairs, usually doomed to end in failure. Male elves were normally depicted as squat and ugly, but their female counterparts were very different. Under moonlight, in particular, elf maidens had a shimmering allure that most men found irresistible. They sang as sweetly as the sirens and their dances were full of grace and sensuality. They always faced their suitors, however, for elves have hollow backs. From behind they resemble trees struck by lightning. There are many stories of young men falling in love with elves. Sometimes they are lured away and never return; if they do, they are damaged in some way: crippled, speechless or befuddled. In their hearts they always remain under the spell of their elf maid.

Froud has reinvigorated the fairy genre, taking it out of the nursery and returning it to the adult world. His work has a particularly strong appeal for New Age enthusiasts, with their interest in Celtic myths, traditional folklore and alternative forms of spiritual belief. Some of his subjects have a medieval flavour, which harks back to the Victorian taste for Arthurian themes, but is also reminiscent of the contemporary movement by the Brotherhood of Ruralists.

❧ A Fairy Verse

Haste thee nymph, and bring with thee
Jest and youthful Jollity,
Quips and Cranks, and wanton Wiles,
Nods, and Becks, and Wreathèd Smiles,
Such as hang on Hebe's cheek,
And love to live in dimple sleek;
John Milton, 'L'Allegro'

The Natural World

he association between fairies and the countryside is very ancient, deriving ultimately from nature religions, which held that every tree, hill and stream had its own protecting spirit. When these cults died away, some of the superstitions became linked with fairies. Thus, traditional sayings such as 'fairy folks are in old oaks' were often based on genuine beliefs.

Nature fairies frequently had specific roles. The Cailleach Bheur (the Celtic Winter fairy), for example, was charged with looking after the deer on Scottish hillsides. In a similar vein, the Light Elves of Scandinavian mythology were expected to care for all plants and flowers. Some of Shakespeare's fairies carried out similar duties, and the importance of their task was emphasized in *A Midsummer Night's Dream*. For, when fairies quarrelled, the natural order was disturbed and the seasons went awry.

The link between fairies and nature was less obvious during the height of the fairy boom, when artists drew most of their inspiration from literature and the theatre. It was gradually restored by Fitzgerald and his successors, who chose to portray diminutive fairies in their natural, microscopic environment. The trend even survived into the twentieth century, when children's artists like Cicely Mary Barker depicted individual fairies with specific flowers and seasons.

Amelia Jane Murray (Lady Oswald)

Born 1800 Port-e-Chee, Isle of Man

Died 1896

A Fairy Resting Among Flowers (right)

As her title suggests, Lady Oswald came from a privileged background. She was the daughter of Lord Henry Murray and spent her formative years on the family estate on the Isle of Man. Girls from this type of background were expected to demonstrate their artistic accomplishments, and usually received extensive private tuition in this field. They were not encouraged to tackle controversial themes, but flowers in particular would have been deemed eminently suitable. Fairies, too, would have seemed a natural choice, particularly as the two themes were increasingly linked together. This is emphasized by a passage in *Jane Eyre* (1847), where Charlotte Bronte (1816–55) described how her heroine 'busied herself in sketching fancy vignettes'. These included a scene of 'an elf sitting in a hedge-sparrow's nest, under a wreath of hawthorn bloom'.

Murray's fairies are pretty, delicate and innocuous, a template that would eventually be adopted by the illustrators of many children's books. This tiny creature holds a spear, in contrast to the thorns prefered by Fitzgerald's warrior fairies, but in her hands it appears to be a decorative accessory, rather than a weapon.

A Fairy Sitting on a Snail (detail)

This whimsical scene resembles a parody of a royal progress. The fairy assumes the regal air of a queen even if her mount is only a snail, and she waves a leaf instead of a fan. For all this, the most remarkable aspect of the painting is Murray's skill at handling the natural-history elements. In this respect her work has obvious affinities with the illustrated books of the period. The scientific displays at the Great Exhibition of 1851 sparked off a wave of interest in the population at large. There was a positive craze for 'botanizing', learning the names of every plant by heart and for collecting interesting natural specimens. These included flowers, which were often pressed into books, as well as different types of fern, lichen, seaweed and shell. Collecting butterflies, moths and birds' eggs also became popular hobbies. Some people even brought live specimens into the home, keeping them in glass vivaria where their natural living conditions could be replicated for study purposes. Publishers were not slow to capitalize on these fads. Scores of books and magazines on natural history were launched on the market, many of them containing colourful prints. Both the snail and the rose in Murray's painting may well have been copied from publications of this kind.

Fairies Floating Downstream in a Peapod (detail)

Throughout her long career, Lady Oswald specialized in depicting tiny fairies dwarfed by the everyday flowers that surrounded them. In each case the flower is depicted with the same loving care as its miniature inhabitants. There is rarely a specific subject in her pictures and, perhaps for this reason, Murray was never ranked alongside the best of the fairy painters. Today she is probably chiefly remembered for a posthumous collection of her work, *A Regency Lady's Faery Bower*, which was first published in 1985.

Murray was undoubtedly influenced by many of the lavishly illustrated flower books that appeared during her lifetime. The authors of these books did not restrict themselves to botanical or horticultural matters, but also sought to link flowers with ancient folklore or spurious symbolism. Within this context it is hardly surprising that books about flowers and fairies began to flourish. Certainly there was no shortage of books offering sources of information. In *The Sentiment of Flowers* (1837) a clergyman called Robert Tyas produced a series of uplifting remarks to accompany each of the flower engravings by James Edwards.

❧ A Fairy Rhyme

Fairy places, fairy things,
Fairy woods where the wild bee wings,
Tiny trees for tiny dames –
These must all be fairy names!

Robert Louis Stevenson, 'The Flowers'

Fritz Zuber-Buhler

Born 1822 Le Locle, Switzerland

Died 1896

The Spirit of the Morning

The vogue for fairy paintings did not extend far beyond the shores of Britain and Ireland. When Continental artists tackled the subject they did not usually relate it to local folk traditions; instead they tended to use the fairy trappings as decorative, fantasy elements. Fritz Zuber-Buhler was a Swiss painter born in Le Locle, who spent much of his career in France. He trained at the Ecole des Beaux-Arts and the Berlin Academy before living for a brief spell in Rome from 1848–49. He went on to become a regular exhibitor at the Salon, showing his work there between 1850 and 1877. Zuber-Buhler painted in a fresh, naturalistic style, tinged with sentimentality. In common with Sophie Anderson (see page 132), many of his pictures are of young women, often in regional dress. He also depicted prettified rural scenes and images of mothers with their children.

John Simmons

Born 1823 Bristol, England

Died 1876

Flying Fairy (detail)

A native of Bristol, Simmons was trained as a miniaturist and earned his living primarily as a portraitist. During the 1860s, however, he found a profitable niche market producing fairy pictures. Most of these followed a set pattern: a moonlit scene with a mildly erotic female nude, posing amidst an array of giant flowers. His work has sometimes been described as pornographic, although tellingly this criticism has largely come from modern critics, rather than Simmons' contemporaries.

Nude paintings could be controversial in the Victorian era. Some commentators felt that displays of this kind were alien to the Anglo-Saxon temperament. In 1867, for example, a critic in the *Art Journal* proclaimed that, "The French do not even pretend to delicacy. Our notions, fortunately for the morals of our people, and certainly for the good manners of society, happen to be different, and so English pictures are for the most part decently draped." Despite this it is worth remembering that Lord Frederic Leighton (1830–96), Sir Edward Poynter (1836–1919) and Sir Lawrence Alma-Tadema (1836–1912), three of the leading figures of the English art establishment, were all renowned for their portrayal of the nude.

FLORENCE VERNON

Flourished 1881–1904

The Fairy Haunt

This lively scene is full of incident, as fairies, birds and bats compete for space in the crowded undergrowth. The image of the fairy haunt altered considerably over the course of the nineteenth century. Just as

the concept of fairies was re-assessed so, too, was the miniature world in which they lived. At the start of the century many people thought of nature as ordered and structured, because it had been created by God and must therefore form part of his divine plan. The findings of Charles Darwin (1809–82), however, cast doubts upon this theory. His emphasis on change and mutation encouraged fairy artists to think again, as did the notion of 'the survival of the fittest', a phrase coined by Herbert Spencer (1820–1903). Some of the strange, insect-like creatures that appear in later fairy paintings may well have been conceived as mutations. Similarly the idyllic settings that had been the natural habitat of some of the earlier spirits were often replaced with miniature battlegrounds, where the fairies had to compete with other species for survival.

Etheline E. Dell

Flourished 1885–1891

Fairies and a Fieldmouse

Dell painted several watercolours on the subject of fairies, most of them loosely based on Shakespearean themes. Here, a group of female fairies pamper a mouse by offering it food and stroking its fur. The bloated mouse is unconvincing and may well have been based on a stuffed specimen. The craft of taxidermy entered a new phase after the 1830s, when improved preservation techniques involving the use of arsenic enabled practitioners of the art to achieve more lifelike results.

The fairies are exclusively female and are reminiscent to a degree of the erotic creations of Simmons. As always with Dell, however, it is the flowers that catch the eye. The gigantic blooms cluster together and press inwards on the scene. On their petals there are dewdrops that dwarf the distant stars. The sheer size of the flowers makes them seem slightly threatening. In this regard Dell probably drew inspiration from botanical illustrations, where there was often a disparity of scale between the flower and its setting. The most celebrated example of this phenomenon dates from the start of the Romantic era when Dr Robert Thornton (1768–1837) produced his *Temple of Flora* (1799–1807). His enormous blooms were set against atmospheric backgrounds so that even the most unpretentious flower could appear distinctly menacing.

Sir Edward Coley Burne-Jones

Born 1833 Birmingham, England

Died 1898

Rainbow Fairy, c. 1890

This tiny watercolour comes from the *Flower Book*, a private project that absorbed the artist in his later years. The book contains 38 circular paintings each representing a single flower. The individual blooms do not appear in these pictures; instead they are evoked through mysterious allegories. In some cases these take the form of elaborate puns, similar to Sidney Harold Meteyard's (1868–1947) *Love in Idleness*. Burne-Jones began the series in 1882 when he created *Love-in-a-Mist*, depicting the figure of Love in a misty landscape. Most of the titles have similarly evocative names, such as *Love in a Tangle*, *Black Archangel* and *Most Bitter Moonseed*. Here the rainbow is probably a reference to the iris, since this took its name from the goddess of the rainbow (see page 63).

Burne-Jones produced the *Flower Book* primarily for his own amusement, giving full rein to his imagination. As a result the pictures have a strong Symbolist flavour, with more emphasis placed on poetic mood than meaning. The painter eventually gave the book to his wife, Georgiana, who described it as "the most soothing piece of work that he ever did". The format proved influential, giving rise to other flower books such as those by Cicely Mary Barker (1895–1973).

Walter Jenks Morgan

Born 1847 Bilston, England

Died 1924

Here I am to Rescue You (detail)

Because of their diminutive size, fairies were vulnerable to attack from many of the other creatures that lived alongside them. Spiders had long been identified as one of their principal enemies. Both Michael Drayton (1563–1631) and Shakespeare included passages in their writings, which highlighted their ongoing attempts to ensnare fairies in their cobwebs, while for their part the fairies hunted spiders for their skins.

Morgan's painting marks a traditional stage in the fairy painters' approach to the natural world. In the mid-nineteenth century, the countryside was often portrayed as a hostile place, where fairies had to battle to survive. By the end of the century, however, as the subject was increasingly geared towards children, sentimentality and cuteness became the order of the day. Morgan managed to produce work in both styles. During his lifetime, he was mainly known as a graphic artist, rather than a painter. After studying at the Birmingham School of Art and the Birmingham Society of Artists, he trained as a lithographer and worked on a variety of popular, illustrated magazines.

✤ A Fairy Verse
It is the season now to go
About the country high and low,
Among the lilacs hand in hand,
And two by two in fairy land.
Robert Louis Stevenson, 'It is the Season'

Arthur Herbert Buckland

Born 1870 Taunton, England

Died 1927

The Fairy and the Beetle, 1922

In many ways, this is the fairy equivalent of Emile Munier's
(1840–95) *The Rescue* (see page 189). In both cases the wings
provided a suitable pretext for producing a sentimental picture of
a child. In Buckland's case, however, there was far more emphasis
on the plein-air setting. There was a vogue for paintings of outdoor
nudes at the turn of the century. In part this was due to the
development of English Impressionism, and in part to public health
issues. There was growing recognition of the value of fresh air and
exercise, which helps to explain the popularity of swimming and
bathing pictures. In addition, the foundation of the Fellowship of
the Naked Trust in 1891 signalled the start of the naturist movement.

    Buckland was born in Taunton, but trained in Paris at the
Académie Julian. He showed his work at both the Royal Academy
and the Paris Salon. Buckland was a highly versatile artist. He was
known primarily for his Romantic landscapes, but also produced
portraits, genre scenes and book illustrations.

Daphne Constance Allen

Born 1899 London, England

Died unknown

Flower Fairies: Spring

This belongs to a set of paintings depicting the four seasons, accompanied by the relevant fairies and flowers (see pages 177–9). The immediate stimulus for the series probably came from the phenomenal success of Cicely Mary Barker's (1895–1973) books on flower fairies. The first of these, *Flower Fairies of*

the Spring, was published in 1923 and proved such a hit that it was rapidly followed into print by similar books on the other seasons. After this Barker went on to produce a number of variations on the theme, among them *A Flower Fairy Alphabet*, *Flower Fairies of the Wayside* and *Flower Fairies of the Trees*. Each book had the same format: on every page there was a picture of a young child holding a single flower, accompanied by a brief, educational poem. The children were modelled on pupils from a nearby school, run by Cicely's sister. They made their own costumes for the project, dressing up in wings made out of gauze and twigs.

FLOWER FAIRIES: SUMMER

This also comes from the series of four paintings showing flower fairies for each of the seasons. It was painted at the end of a long-lasting trend, which extended back to the mid-Victorian period. The initial popularity of the theme owed much to a general growth of interest in gardening. This had long been the preserve of the rich, but the nineteenth century witnessed the arrival of a new phenomenon: the amateur gardener in the suburbs. They followed the lead of an extraordinary couple, John Loudon (1783–1843) and his wife Jane (1807–58).

He founded several gardening magazines and published an enormous *Encyclopaedia of Gardening*, which became the fount of all knowledge for every amateur. Jane was possibly even more influential. After publishing a fantasy novel in her youth (*The Mummy*, 1827), she produced a marvellous range of gardening books aimed specifically at women. Among others they included *The Ladies' Companion to the Flower Garden* and *Gardening for Ladies*. These books were full of detailed illustrations, which certainly influenced some of the female fairy painters. For the following generation, Gertrude Jekyll was equally important. She was a regular contributor to *Country Life* and the *Garden*.

Flower Fairies: Autumn

Depictions of the four seasons had been common since antiquity and were frequently used in decorative schemes. Over the years, a set of symbols evolved to represent these, some of which were adopted by Allen. Spring was normally portrayed as a young girl with flowers; the depiction of summer included signs of harvesting, such as a sickle or a sheaf of corn; autumn featured grapes and vine leaves; while winter showed people wrapped up warmly against the cold.

The fairy with the cobweb may well have been inspired by one of Titania's attendants in *A Midsummer Night's Dream*. Some of the latter were associated with plants, although more importantly they were also linked with healing, another fairy skill. Mustard seed was one of the ingredients used in poultices for stiff muscles; boiled moths were employed in a number of plasters and potions; the pea plant (as in Peaseblossom) was said to relieve the melancholy effects of lost love; while cobwebs were often placed on cuts, to help staunch any bleeding.

Flower Fairies: Winter

This is the last of the series of paintings showing flower fairies at various times of the year. For obvious reasons, winter presented the artist with the greatest difficulties. In the absence of flowers, she decided to focus on the friendship between fairies and birds, presenting a far more harmonious view of their relationship than most of the earlier fairy painters.

Daphne Allen was born in London and taught to paint by her father, who was also an artist. She displayed a precocious talent, exhibiting her paintings from the age of 13. While still a teenager she also contributed to two books, *A Child's Visions* and *The Birth of the Opal*. These early efforts gained considerable attention in the press, where Allen was described as a prodigy. Her adult career never quite lived up to this early promise, but she became a prolific illustrator, producing work for the *Illustrated London News*, the *Tatler* and the *Sketch*. As a painter she was probably best known for her religious works. The most notable of these were commissioned for the reredos at Christ Church Cathedral in Newcastle, Australia.

Angels & Religion

or the art-going public of the Victorian era, pictures of beautiful winged creatures were a familiar sight. Paintings of fairies, angels, cupids and cherubs filled the walls of exhibition galleries and museums. In theory, these pictures should have been very different, as they stemmed from fields that hardly seemed compatible – Christianity, pagan mythology and fantasy. In practice, though, the boundaries between these concepts had become rather blurred. It was just as acceptable to place a fairy on top of a Christmas tree as it was to use an angel; and in pantomimes, the fairy godmother had become the popular equivalent of a guardian angel.

In artistic terms, angels came from far older traditions than fairies. They took their name from *angelos*, a Greek word for 'messenger', and derived some aspects of their appearance from the winged messenger-spirits of Assyrian sculpture. Cherubs were at first shown as a head surrounded by three pairs of wings based on the descriptions in Ezekiel

and Isaiah, but artists soon preferred to depict them as winged infants. Cupid, the god of love, was portrayed as a youth in certain themes, most notably his affair with Psyche. When he was shown with Venus, however, he was usually depicted as a child. In addition, both of these deities were occasionally accompanied by winged infants, who acted as their attendants. In purely visual terms, these are often indistinguishable from the cherubs that were featured in many religious paintings.

Alexandre Cabanel

Born 1823 Montpelier, France

Died 1889

Expulsion from Paradise (detail), (right)

In Cabanel's depiction of the expulsion of Adam and Eve, God has arrived in the Garden of Eden, ready to deliver his judgment on the sinful couple. He is accompanied by the cherubim, who will guard the entrance to Paradise, to prevent Adam and Eve from returning. In addition to their function as divine protectors, cherubims were sometimes shown bearing God on their wings. Several references to this can be found in the Bible, among them a passage in the Book of Samuel: 'And He rode upon a cherub, and did fly: and He was seen upon the wings of the wind' (II Samuel XXII, 11).

Cabanel was a successful Salon artist, who built his reputation on his skill at portraying the human figure. It is no surprise, therefore, that he chose the nude studies of Adam and Eve as the main focus of this painting. Eve, in particular, appears under the spotlight. Cabanel portrayed her in the same manner as his mythological characters so that she resembles a startled nymph or goddess. In spite of his immense popularity, the artist's fame faded swiftly following his death.

❧ A Fairy Song
In this dim world of clouding cares,
We rarely know, till 'wildered eyes
See white wings lessening up the skies
The angels with us unawares.
Gerald Massey, 'Ballad of Babe Christabel'

William Adolphe Bouguereau

Born 1825 La Rochelle, France

Died 1905

Wounded Eros, 1857

This painting combines two popular artistic themes. The subject of a boy removing a thorn from his foot was known from a much-copied antique statue that Bouguereau, as a Classically trained artist, would certainly have known. Thorns also had a particular relevance for Venus and Cupid, both of whom were associated with roses. The second theme, which derived originally from one of the *Idylls* by Theocritus, showed the love god suffering after he had been stung by a bee. Most versions showed the boy standing tearfully beside his mother, holding the honeycomb that he had tried to steal. This anecdote was usually portrayed as a moral fable, as Venus pointed out to her child that the wounds he inflicted with his bow and arrows caused just as much distress to his victims.

Sir Edward Coley Burne-Jones

Born 1833 Birmingham, England

Died 1898

The Annunciation (The Flower of God) (detail), 1862

Over the course of his career, Burne-Jones tackled this subject many times and it is a tribute to his skill that he managed to bring something new to each version. On this occasion the most extraordinary feature is the setting, with the virgin kneeling in the upper floor of a modest, wooden building, while Gabriel perches on the branches of a tree. Christian artists often depicted Mary in a dark, crumbling edifice, indicating that she was raised in the old, Judaic order, while the new dispensation is represented by the shaft of light, which streams in through the window. The biblical text on the bed is a traditional feature, while the discarded shoes confirm that this is a sacred event. They refer to a passage in the Book of Exodus, 'Put off thy shoes from off thy feet, for the place whereon thou standest is holy ground'.

Much of Burne-Jones's religious output stemmed from his links with the firm of Morris and Co. Founded by William Morris (1834–96), this remarkable organization sought to revive traditional standards of craftsmanship by leading the drive against shoddy, mass-produced goods. Many of their commissions came from churches.

Constantin Makowsky

Born 1839 Russia

Died 1915

The Toilet of Venus

This subject had been in circulation since the Renaissance, becoming particularly popular in Venice. It survived into the nineteenth century largely because the subject matter was so vague. It was not attached to any specific story from mythology, so artists tended to use it as a pretext for producing a decorative picture of a female nude. Traditionally in a *Toilet of Venus*, the nude was shown reclining, but in Makowsky's version the goddess is enthroned, a pose normally reserved for a *Triumph of Venus*.

The goddess is accompanied by several of her attributes. The most common of these is the mirror, a conventional symbol for vanity or lust. In Renaissance allegories Venus was often portrayed as a personification of lust, although later artists preferred to link her with *voluptas* or 'pleasure'. As usual she is surrounded by *amoretti* (the diminutive form of amor or 'love'), and these chubby figures act as playful reminders of the identity of the goddess. Amidst the profusion of flowers there are many roses, a plant that was sacred to Venus. The inclusion of a peacock in such a prominent position is a surprise, since the bird was traditionally associated with the goddess Juno. Here it may represent Pride.

> ❧ A Fairy Song
>
> Sea-born goddess, let me be
> By thy son thus graced, and thee,
> That whene'er I woo, I find
> Virgins coy, but not unkind.
>
> Robert Herrick,
> 'A Hymn to Venus and Cupid'

Eugène Medard

Born 1847 France

Died 1887

L'Amour et Psyche ('Cupid and Psyche'), 1878

This tangled tale revolved around Psyche, a young maiden whose beauty won her great renown. It even aroused the jealousy of Venus, who sent her son, Cupid, to unleash one of his arrows at the girl so that she would become infatuated with some hideous creature. This cruel plot backfired, however, and Cupid himself fell in love with her. He installed Psyche in his palace and came to her chamber every night under cover of darkness. He also forbade her to try and look upon his face. Psyche soon fell under the spell of this mysterious stranger, but was fearful of his insistence on secrecy. Eventually her curiosity got the better of her and she lit her lamp. Unfortunately a drop of hot oil fell on Cupid's skin, waking him instantly. He was furious at her disobedience and immediately flew off. Here Medard illustrates her vain attempt to hold him back.

Because of its ancient origins, most artists tended to depict this story in a Classical manner, laying particular emphasis on the study of the nude form. This version, however, is more akin to the Romantic fantasies about knights and damsels. Even the silhouette of Cupid's palace resembles a medieval castle.

William Adolphe Bouguereau

Born 1825 La Rochelle, France

Died 1905

L'Innocence, 1890

Towards the end of the nineteenth century there was a vogue for
portraying allegorical pictures of young women. In most cases artists
preferred to depict the most extreme forms of behaviour. Either
the women were paragons of virtue, as in this case, or they were
manifestations of evil, represented by a *femme fatale*. Here, the
subject is Innocence. Her purity is symbolized by her white dress.
She also resists temptation by ignoring the two cherubs, who are
trying to whisper thoughts of love into her ears.

In many ways, Bouguereau was the archetypal establishment
figure in the French art world. He won the Prix de Rome in 1850,
the award most coveted by young academic artists, and for almost
30 years (1876–1905) he was on the governing body of the Académie
des Beaux-Arts. This institution had enormous influence, organizing
the exhibitions at the Salon, supervising education and advising
on state commissions. By reputation it was fiercely conservative,
opposing the Impressionists and most other avant-garde trends.
Paul Cézanne (1839–1906), for example, expressed his regret at
being barred from the 'Salon of Monsieur Bouguereau'. As a bastion
of authority, Bouguereau's reputation plummeted after his death,
although critics have acknowledged his technical skill.

L'Amour Mouillé, 1890

Like Peter Pan, Cupid never grew up. Even though some of the stories associated with him have a fairly adult theme – the legend of Cupid and Psyche is an obvious example – he was increasingly portrayed as a young child. By the nineteenth century there was also a growing tendency to use Classical accessories as nothing more than decorative trappings. Here, for example, there is no obvious story line. Bouguereau simply wanted to produce an attractive picture of a youngster.

The idealization of children in art and literature went hand in hand with a growing interest in their welfare. The Industrial Revolution brought with it a dependency on child labour, particularly in the mines and the cotton mills. Attempts were made to redress this situation in the early Victorian period. One of the principal reformers was the 7th Earl of Shaftesbury (1801–85), who was instrumental in passing the Factory Acts (1833–50) and the Mines Act (1842), which restricted the use of children. Fittingly, when a monument was created in his honour, it took the form of a statue of Eros, the name for the Greek god that the Romans later referred to as Cupid. This famous landmark is situated next to Shaftesbury Avenue in London, the street that was named after him.

✤ A Fairy Song
May Cupid's shafts by love imprest
Smile sweetly soothing in thy breast
Inspiring ardent love for me
As pure and true as mine for thee
Victorian song

Emile Munier

Born 1840 Paris, France

Died 1895

Le Sauvetage ('The Rescue'), 1894

Sentimental pictures of young children were extremely popular in the late nineteenth century, whether in a domestic setting or in the guise of figures from the past. Here, two youngsters are portrayed as mischievous cupids. They have been larking about near the river and a quiver of arrows has fallen in the water.

Munier's father was an upholsterer and at the start of his career he followed a similar path, working at the Gobelins, a famous tapestry factory. He switched to painting after becoming interested in the work of François Boucher (1703–70), a Rococo artist who had produced designs for the Gobelins. He was also inspired by the example of Bouguereau (see page 187), who became his friend and mentor. The latter nicknamed him 'sage Munier' ('Munier the wise'). He adopted the same highly polished style as Bouguereau, although his subject matter was quite different – by the 1880s he was specializing in paintings of children and animals. Munier's two children, Henri and Marie-Louise, served as models for many of these pictures. His most successful work in this vein was *Three Friends*, featuring a child, a kitten and a dog, which became famous after Pears Soap used it in one of their advertising campaigns.

Gabriel-Joseph-Marie-Augustin Ferrier

Born 1847 France

Died 1914

L'Ange Gardien ('The Guardian Angel')

The concept of the guardian angel was derived from a few biblical references. In the Gospel of St Matthew, Christ mentions how the 'little ones' have 'their angels (who) do always behold the face' of God (Matthew XVIII, 10). There is also a specific example in the Book of Tobit, in the Apocrypha, where Raphael acts as the guardian angel of Tobias. The idea was taken up by the Catholic Church: several popes introduced specific feast days for 'our guardian angels', and in a number of Baroque churches there are special chapels dedicated to them.

In artistic terms the subject evolved from early depictions of death scenes. These would often portray the soul as a naked infant being lifted out of the body and carried up to heaven by a small angel. These images strengthened the association between children and guardian angels, although in purely doctrinal terms the Church made it clear that adults also had their spiritual protectors. Nevertheless, nineteenth-century depictions of the subject were usually focused on infants, in part no doubt because of the health risks that they faced.

Ferrier is mainly remembered now as a teacher rather than for his own work. His best-known pupil was the Cubist artist Fernand Léger (1881–1955).

John William Waterhouse

Born 1849 Rome, Italy

Died 1917

The Annunciation, 1914

The Pre-Raphaelites and their successors tried to instil a greater sense of realism into their religious pictures. In doing so they were following the advice of the critic, John Ruskin (1819–1900), who urged painters to portray the virgin as 'a simple Jewish girl', rather than 'a graceful princess crowned with gems'.

Waterhouse's remarkable version of the subject certainly breathed new life into the theme, avoiding many of the old clichés. He portrays the virgin as a young woman rather than a sacred icon. Her pose is very natural, reflecting her obvious surprise at seeing an angel appear out of nowhere. The setting is presented in an equally novel fashion, even though it manages to include several of the customary symbols. Traditionally the virgin is kneeling at a *prie-dieu* when Gabriel arrives. On it there is a text from the Old Testament prophesying the coming of the Saviour. Often, as here, there is a distaff (a stick for spinning thread) by the virgin's side. This alludes to the legend that Mary was raised at the Temple in Jerusalem, where she made vestments for the priests.

Edward A. Fellowes-Prynne

Born 1854 England

Died 1921

Ecce Ancilla Domini

This sumptuously coloured version of the Annunciation follows a traditional format, employing a symbolic formula that had been in use since the Middle Ages. The archangel Gabriel arrives on a cloud, bringing Mary the news that she has been chosen by God to be the mother of Christ. His words are also shown on a strip of material, which hangs from his costume, '*Ave gratis plena Dominus tecum*' ('Greetings most favoured one! The Lord is with you', Luke I:28). The virgin, meanwhile, holds her hand to her breast and utters the words "*Ecce ancilla domini*" ("Here I am. I am the Lord's servant", Luke I:38) thereby accepting her destiny. At the top of the picture a ray of light beams down from the dove, which symbolizes the Holy Spirit.

The light itself represents the Incarnation of Christ. When the beam touches her head, this is the moment of conception. Mary's purity is symbolized both by the lily and by the fence behind her. This indicates that she is standing in a *hortus conclusus* ('enclosed garden'), a traditional symbol of virginity. On the right-hand side, the apple on the wall refers to the temptation of Eve. Mary was described by theologians as the second Eve, because of her part in bringing about the redemption of humanity.

Henry Siddons Mowbray

Born 1858 Alexandria, Egypt

Died 1928

The Marriage of Persephone (detail)

According to Greek mythology, Persephone was the daughter of Zeus and Demeter. One day she was out in the fields picking flowers with her friends when she caught the eye of Pluto, the god of the underworld. He had just been struck by one of Cupid's arrows and was immediately captivated by her beauty. Gathering her up in his chariot, he opened a chasm in the earth's surface and swept her off to Hades, his subterranean domain. Demeter, the corn goddess who ensured continual summer, was inconsolable at her daughter's disappearance. In her grief she let the fields become barren and no crops grew. Seeing this, Zeus gave orders for a compromise. Persephone was to be returned, provided she had eaten nothing during her captivity. Unfortunately for the unwilling bride she had consumed six pomegranate seeds and was thus only allowed to surface for six months of the year, which were to become spring and summer. For the remainder she was obliged to return to the underworld, during which autumn and winter would occur.

This picture illustrates Persephone leaving her friends to rejoin her husband. She is led to him by Hermes, shown with the winged helmet, who traditionally escorted the dead to Hades. In spite of the relationship's reluctant nature, Persephone was frequently depicted with symbols of love, such as Cupid and winged cherubic *amoretti*.

Hans Zatzka

Born 1859 Vienna, Austria

Died 1945

The Birth of Venus

In Zatzka's playful scene, Love is personified by the goddess Venus. She was traditionally associated with the scallop shell as a result of the legend that she was born out of the sea and carried ashore on a giant shell. Many artists portrayed this subject, most famously Botticelli (c. 1445–1510) in his *Birth of Venus* (c. 1485), and some also depicted the shell as a type of boat drawn by swans. Here Zatzka has turned it into a bed, transforming the surrounding riverside scene into a romantic, open-air boudoir. Venus is surrounded by some of her traditional attributes. Roses are scattered everywhere, referring to the myth that she helped create the first red rose. Similarly the profusion of other flowers relates to the legend that after she first set foot on dry land, flowers sprang up in her footsteps. The frolicking *putti*, who hover in the air, are also a predictable feature. Only the fairy strikes an incongruous note. Fairy painting was very much an English tradition, which had little impact on the other side of the Channel. When they were included in French pictures, fairies were often used rather indiscriminately as a fantasy element in any mythical scene.

William Henry Margetson

Born 1861 London, England

Died 1940

The Stranger

This type of study became popular in the late nineteenth century, when there was a taste for pictures that hinted at a story but did not offer a firm narrative. Here a woman sits in a reflective mood with Cupid at her feet. She is so wrapped up in her thoughts that she has lost interest in her book and does not appear to notice the god of love as he offers her a rose. By ignoring Cupid's gift there is a suggestion that she is the stranger in the title, a stranger to love.

Margetson studied at the South Kensington Schools and the Royal Academy, where he began exhibiting in 1885. He specialized in rather wistful studies of women on their own, usually cast in a vaguely allegorical or mythological setting. Some of these were adapted for use as advertising posters. He also produced a few religious pictures, most notably St Mary at the Loom.

Guillaume Seignac

Born 1870 France

Died 1924

The Wings of Desire

Although known as the Roman god of love, Cupid is linked more specifically with desire (the Latin word cupido means 'desire'). Similarly, when humanist philosophers wrote about Cupid and Psyche, they described them as an allegory of the union between Desire (Cupid) and the Soul (Psyche), which produced Pleasure as its offspring. In artistic terms, the status of Cupid was often downgraded. Venus was seen as the presiding deity of love and he was cast in the role of her son or one of her attendants. This role is emphasized here by the red roses that adorn his hair. These blooms were sacred to Venus and were one of her chief attributes. This stems from the legend that the first red rose was created when she pricked her foot on a thorn and stained a white rose crimson with her blood.

In nineteenth-century art, painters often used the theme of Cupid simply as a pretext for portraying a pretty child. The celebration of childhood was a new development. Children featured prominently in the novels of Charles Dickens (1812–70) and Mark Twain (1835–1910), while artists illustrated scenes from their everyday lives. Sentimental images such as this were often copied as oleographs or tapestries and hung in the family home.

❧ A Fairy Rhyme

Cupid laid by his brand, and fell asleep:
A maid of Dian's this advantage found,
And his love-kindling fire did quickly steep
In a cold valley-fountain of that ground;
Which borrow'd from this holy fire of Love ...
William Shakespeare,
'Sonnet CLIII'

L'Amour Désarmé ('Cupid Disarmed') (detail)

This light-hearted scene illustrates the way that mythological subjects were popularized for the general market. Cupid is shown in the guise of a naughty infant, who has been causing trouble with his bow and arrow. As a result, Venus has decided to confiscate the weapons and attempts to conceal them behind her back. Seignac's picture is in a conventional academic style, although the frivolous mood is more reminiscent of the Rococo period a century earlier.

As a theme, the punishment of Cupid has a long pedigree. Over the years many of the Classical gods were featured in the scene, although Venus, as Cupid's mother, was usually the figure of authority. Sometimes she pulls the weapons away from the boy, while elsewhere she threatens to chastise him with a bunch of roses. Cupid's amorous escapades also aroused the anger of Diana, the chaste goddess of the hunt. On some occasions her nymphs were pictured in the act of breaking or burning the arrows while the child lay sleeping. Mars, the god of war, was also depicted in a similar vein, often trying to clip the infant's wings. His attempts at discipline were sometimes thwarted, however, as artists tried to combine the punishment with the equally popular theme of love overcoming strife.

CREDITS

Courtesy of Bridgeman Art Library:

© Art Gallery and Museum, Kelvingrove, Glasgow, Scotland, Glasgow City Council (Museums) 1, 33; © Chris Beetles, London, UK 174; © Chris Beetles, London, UK/Charles James Folkard 142; © Christie's Images, London, UK 81; © Christopher Wood Gallery, London, UK 106–9, 119, 145; © Fairy Art Museum, Tokyo, Japan 173; © Fitzwilliam Museum, University of Cambridge, UK 82; © Leeds Museums and Galleries (Lotherton Hall), UK 160; © National Gallery of Scotland, Edinburgh, Scotland 5, 25, 26, 112; © Newport Museum and Art Gallery, South Wales 70; © Private Collection 14, 15, 21, 38, 40, 76, 122, 130; © Private Collection/Chris Beetles, London, UK/Arthur Rackham 88, 89; © Private Collection/Arthur Rackham 92; © Private Collection/Christopher Wood Gallery, London, UK 153; © Private Collection/The Fine Art Society, London, UK 24, 28; © Private Collection/The Stapleton Collection 73; © Roy Miles Fine Paintings 158; © Sheffield Galleries and Museums Trust, UK 30; © The Makins Collection 116; © The Mass Gallery, London, UK 10–13, 18, 35, 39, 41, 43, 44, 49, 57, 58, 75, 115, 132, 134, 149, 151, 156, 169; © The Stapleton Collection 45, 71; © The Sullivan Collection 111; © University of Liverpool Art Gallery & Collections, UK/Arthur Rackham 94; © Victoria & Albert Museum, London, UK 131; © Victoria & Albert Museum, London, UK/Edmund Dulac 143; © Victoria & Albert Museum, London, UK/The Stapleton Collection 133; © Victoria & Albert Museum, London, UK/The Stapleton Collection/Arthur Rackham 96; © Walker Art Gallery, Liverpool, Merseyside, UK, National Museums Liverpool 46; © Yale Centre for British Art, Paul Mellon Fund, USA 29.

Courtesy of Christie's Images Ltd: 6–9, 16, 19, 37, 48, 50–52, 54, 56, 61, 72, 74, 78, 80, 83, 114, 117, 120, 129, 150, 157, 164–7, 170–1, 180–1, 183, 185, 187, 193, 197; © John McKirdy Duncan 141; © William Henry Margetson 195; © NYC Christie's Images Ltd 189; © Arthur Rackham 86, 102, 105.

Courtesy of Mary Evans Picture Library: © Warwick Goble 140, 146; © Arthur Rackham 84–5, 87, 90–1, 93, 97–9, 101, 103–4.

Courtesy of Sotheby's Picture Library: 3, 27, 34, 42, 53, 55, 60, 62, 65–6, 69, 77, 113, 121, 124–6, 128, 138–9, 154, 159, 168, 172, 176–9, 182, 186, 188, 190–2, 196; © Estella Louisa Michaela Canziani 161; © Joyce Dennys 147; © Brian Froud 137, 163; © Grace Jones 162; © Arthur Rackham 100; © Hans Zatzka 194.

Courtesy of Tate, London: 22–3, 110.

© Jean & Ron Henry 2005 136.

The Arthur Rackham pictures are reproduced with the kind permission of his family.

Author: Iain Zaczek

Iain Zaczek was born in Dundee, Scotland, and educated at Wadham College, Oxford, and the Courtauld Institute of Art. He has since gone on to forge an impressive career as a freelance writer on art- and Celtic-related subjects, and is interested in particular in Pre-Raphaelite art and International Gothic. Recent publications include *Essential Art Deco, The Essential William Morris, The Art of the Icon, Lovers in Art* and *Impressive Interiors*.

Index